THE LOTHIAN CRAFT SERIES

The Candle Book

Pamela Allardice

Lothian
BOOKS

DEDICATION

For my sons Edward and Randall, who 'helped' me make the candles in this book.

Thomas C. Lothian Pty Ltd
11 Munro Street, Port Melbourne, Victoria 3207

First published 1996
Copyright © Pamela Allardice 1996

All rights reserved. No part of this publication may be reproduced, stored in a retrieval system or transmitted in any form by any process without the prior permission of the copyright holder. Enquiries should be made to the publisher.

National Library of Australia
Cataloguing-in-Publication data:

Allardice, Pamela, 1958–
  The Candle Book.

  Includes index.
  ISBN 0 85091 745 X

  1. Candlemaking. I. Title. (Series: Lothian craft series).

745.59332

Cover design by Modern Art Production Group
Text design by Jo Waite Design
Illustrations by Julia McLeish
Photography by Bill Thomas
Printed by PT Pac-Rim Kwartanusa Printing, Indonesia

Contents

INTRODUCTION 4
History of candlemaking and use, and traditions.

GETTING STARTED 8
* Wax * Stearin * Wicks * Dyes
* Scents * Scales and measuring jug
* Saucepans and spoons
* Thermometer * Wicking needles
* Moulds * Mould seal
* Other equipment * Top tips for a professional finish

CANDLES TO MAKE 23
How to make tapered, moulded and rolled candles. Dipping. How to decorate candles, by appliqué, painting, stencilling.

* Ice Candle 23
* Sand Candle 24
* Dipped Candle 26
* Twisted Candle 28
* Painted Candles 29
* Floating Candles 31
* Stencilled Candles 33
* Rose candle 34
* Pressed Flower Candle 36
* Lavender Candle 39
* Herb Candle 41
* Eggshell Candle 42
* Studded Candle 43
* Jewelled Candle 44
* Christmas Tree Candle 45
* Mosaic Candle 46
* Medieval Candle 48
* Shell Candles 51
* Beeswax Candles 52
* Starry Candles 54
* Treasure Candles 55

CANDLE HOLDERS 59
How to make unusual candle holders and moulds.

* Pine Cone Ring 59
* Flower Pots 59
* Decorated Tin Cans 60
* Ivy Garlands 60
* Floral Pedestal 60
* Glasses 61
* Bottles 61

Resources 62
Recommended Reading 63
Index 64

Introduction

THE CANDLE IS ONE of the oldest answers to the problem of supplying light after darkness falls. A number of changes have been made to methods of candle manufacture, and today, through the variety of moulds now available, we have a wonderful selection of shapes to choose from, but there is no basic difference between a candle made in the past and one made today.

The idea of wrapping a waxy substance around a wick is a very ancient one, with references to lighting candles and rush lights occurring as early as 3000 BC in Crete and Egypt. Candles are mentioned in Biblical writings as early as the tenth century BC, and a fragment of candle dating from the first century AD has been found in Avignon, France. Candlesticks, not unlike some of our modern candleholders in appearance, have been found in ruins in Crete, and date back to 30 centuries before the birth of Jesus Christ.

The ancient Roman writer the younger Pliny gives us a vivid picture of his home outside Tuscany, around 100 AD, describing the terrace scented with violets and the outdoor pool. Food was served on the marble edge of the pool, and the lighter dishes of food were floated towards the diners in vessels shaped like birds or little boats. When night fell on the villa, the whole enchanted scene was lit by small lamps made of pottery or bronze, with a hole for the wick and another to replenish the oil, as well as candles in pottery candlesticks and iron candle holders. How romantic!

We also know candles were used in the great halls, monasteries and churches of medieval times, as well as being used to light cottages and shops. In the time of English King Alfred, torches stuck in the walls supplied lighting, but those who could afford them used candles as well as lanterns made of ox-horn. The simplest – and probably smelliest – candle of all was the rush light, made by dipping rushes in melted leftover kitchen fat.

In Wales, the tradition of using rush lights like these lingered right up until the early part of this century. It is still traditional in several areas for village women and children to gather rushes from the banks of streams in late summertime as part of a seasonal celebration, even though the lights are no longer used or made.

Special angled holders were used to hold rush lights, and tiresome things they must have been, burning for only 15–20 minutes each, and so needing constant attention to maintain light. Yet women still managed to sew and embroider, even by the dim light of candles and

Rush light holder

rush lights. Sometimes, if they could not afford candles, they worked by the light of the fire. This was called 'keeping blindman's holiday'.

For many centuries in Europe, candles were an expensive item. Those who could afford them bought town-made candles from the wax-chandler or from itinerant salesmen and gipsies. These candles were made of wax or tallow (animal fat) and were placed in silver, wooden or pewter candlesticks, which were sometimes 3 metres tall and held several candles. Hanging candelabra of brass, wood or iron were suspended from the ceiling by pulleys, ropes and chains.

From the sixteenth century onwards, living standards improved throughout society and even poor people were able to afford to use candles every day, as evidenced by the increasing availability of candlesticks and candleholders from this time, and their appearance in household registries. But even if they owned several manors and much land, lords of the manor seem to have been cautious with ready cash.

A certain Lady Margaret Paston had to write to her husband in London in 1499 saying that she was down to her last four candles and would have to borrow money unless he came home soon.

At this time, candles were usually sold by the pound and were bundled in eights, tens or twelves (the thinnest). Candles for everyday use were made of tallow, which is simply animal fat, usually from sheep (mutton) or cows. Mutton tallow was preferred as it was the hardest. And in the home, surplus fat from cooking was saved in the kitchen, and one of the many tasks of the housewife – and probably a pretty awful one by today's standards! – was making candles:

The careful wife of an industrious Hampshire labourer obtains all her fat for nothing; for she saves the scummings of her bacon pot for this use; and, if the grease abounds with salt, she causes the salt to precipitate to the bottom, by setting the scummings in a warm oven. Where hogs were not much in use, and especially by the sea-side, the coarser animal-oils will come very cheap. A pound of common grease may be procured for four pence.

Gilbert White, *Natural History of Selbourne,* 1789

These candles were usually dark, yellowish in colour, and probably gave off a pretty nasty smell. In farming communities, it usually fell to the farmers' wives to make candles at home, along with butter, cheese, beer and many other everyday necessities. Given her workload, and the general unpleasantness of the task, it is not surprising that candlemakers, or 'chandlers' became widespread from the early eighteenth century.

In England both the wax chandlers and the tallow chandlers formed their own guilds. By the thirteenth century the French had also established separate guilds for wax and tallow chandlers, and the same course was followed in London. The Worshipful Company of

Candles play an important role in all rituals to do with death and the passing of life, and candles are often burned continuously by a coffin lying in state before burial. This symbolises the Holy Spirit guarding the corpse, and stems from the days when it was thought a lighted candle could chase away evil spirits who might have stolen the corpse.

Wax Chandlers was incorporated in 1484. The insignia of the company shows three red roses on a white chevron divided by three squat 'prickets', being the candles set on metal spikes and used in mortuaries, rather than those set into shallow cups. The English Tallow Chandlers were probably of equal antiquity, and were incorporated as a company in 1462. As the name suggests, they regulated trade in candles made from animal fats, although for a time during the reign of Elizabeth I they also controlled sales of soap, hops, vinegar and oil.

It was quite common to find the trades of soap manufacture and candlemaking combined, as both used tallow and vegetable oils. For instance, in 1754, in the then rapidly growing city of New York, USA, John Ditcher offered his services in these words:

He makes Candles and Soap for those who are pleas'd to find their own Tallow at reasonable rates; said Ditcher has his own Tools well fix'd after the London Manner. He would be glad of a partner with a little Cash.

Interestingly, the wax chandlers were considered more genteel than the tallow ones – and their business was more profitable, for people were prepared to pay more for a wax candle. As time went by the use of candles became even more widespread, and in 1740 England's Queen Anne introduced a tax on candles. It amounted to fourpence a pound on wax candles and a halfpenny a pound on tallow candles. Still, despite the enforcing of successive versions of this Act, considerable evasion took place!

Until several hundred years ago, candles were still the most widespread form of lighting known. The quality of light depended upon the type of material used to make the candle: beeswax, for instance, gave off a much brighter light than did the more common – and smelly – tallow. Both materials had been familiar to humankind for centuries. Then, in addition to tallow and beeswax, another material became popular for candlemaking around this time – spermaceti. This was a hard white waxy substance derived from the oil present in the head cavities of sperm whales. These candles were highly prized, for they burned with a very bright white light – so bright, in fact, that a spermaceti candle flame was taken as a standard light measure for photometry (the science of light measurement).

Sperma Ceti Candles, exceeding all others for Beauty, Sweetness of Scent when extinguished; Duration, being more than double Tallow Candles of equal size; Dimensions of Flame, nearly four Times more, emitting a soft easy expanding Light, bringing the Object close to the Sight, rather than causing the Eye to take after them, as all Tallow-Candles do, from a constant Dimness which they produce – One of these Candles serves the Use and Purpose of three Tallow Ones, and upon the whole are much pleasanter and cheaper.

News-letter, Boston, Massachusetts, 30 March 1748

Spermaceti candles were slightly cheaper than beeswax candles, and the wax was often mixed with tallow to produce a whiter candle. These candles are no longer made, because of environmental concerns.

The nineteenth century also brought widespread technological innovation, including the development of patented candlemaking machines, ensuring that cheap candles could light even the poorest homes. In England a new law was passed that actually forbade the making of candles at home, unless a special licence was purchased, presumably in an attempt to protect this fledgling industry.

It was also at this time that a significant discovery was made by a chemist, Michel Eugene Chevreul. He had been researching the composition and uses of tallow and found that, instead of being one substance as had been assumed for many centuries, it was actually *two* fatty acids – stearic acid and oleic acid – combined with glycerine to form a neutral non-flammable material.

By removing the glycerine from the tallow mixture, Chrevreul invented a new substance which he named 'stearine', which was harder than tallow and burned with a brighter flame. It was this substance, known today as stearin or stearic acid (see pages 10–11), that led to improved candle quality. It also made candles more economical, as it was harder and so took longer to burn. With the introduction of stearin for candlemaking, it was also possible to make improvements in the manufacture of wicks and end the constant round of snuffing and trimming wicks once candles were lit (see pages 32–3). Instead of being made of simply twisted strands of cotton, wicks were now plaited tightly: the burned portion curled over and was completely consumed, rather than falling messily in the melting wax.

More improvements in commercial candle manufacture followed, including the addition of lime to make high quality hard, white candles, the use of a substance called palmatine, which was derived from palm oil, for candlemaking, and the introduction of the new 'snuffless' candle to coincide with Queen Victoria's wedding to her dear Albert.

Another material for making candles, paraffin wax, was added to the known animal and vegetable sources around 1850. Paraffin wax was first extracted from crude oil. Paraffin wax candles equalled beeswax and spermaceti candles for brightness and hardness, and were even cheaper again. The use of paraffin wax saw the rapid development of petroleum manufacturing and industry in the Pennsylvania oilfields around that time, which yielded huge supplies of this relatively inexpensive material. Paraffin wax is still widely used today in commercial candlemaking, and it is a cheaper alternative to beeswax for your own candlemaking experiments.

Getting Started

*Have you ever heard the expression **'Fine as the king's candle'**? It refers to the ancient custom of presenting, on 6 January, a candle of various colours at a shrine of the three kings of Cologne in Germany. Oddly, the saying is generally used to describe someone who is overdressed, especially a woman wearing lots of ribbons or flowers.*

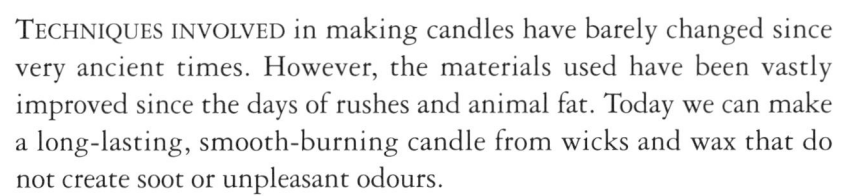

TECHNIQUES INVOLVED in making candles have barely changed since very ancient times. However, the materials used have been vastly improved since the days of rushes and animal fat. Today we can make a long-lasting, smooth-burning candle from wicks and wax that do not create soot or unpleasant odours.

To take up candlemaking as a hobby – or even for profit – you really only need a minimum of equipment and a simple place to work. If you are planning to supply all the local markets with candles, you would need a workshop or special studio with a stove and hot running water, but otherwise the kitchen bench is fine. I tend to spread out whenever I'm making candles and use not only the kitchen bench but also the breakfast table. Candlemaking can be messy, so it's wise to protect both your work surfaces and the floor with plenty of old newspapers.

WAX

Candle wax is readily available at larger art and craft shops and craft suppliers; see Resources on pages 62. Some shops and manufacturers will supply direct mail order but remember that wax is heavy, and postage may be surprisingly expensive. The most commonly used waxes are paraffin wax and beeswax.

Paraffin wax is less expensive, making it a preferred choice for the first-time candlemaker. It is uncoloured and odourless, and is usually sold in easy-to-use flakes or a large solid block, from which you cut off what you need.

Paraffin wax is solid at room temperature and melts at 57–60°C (135–140°F). It may be used alone – indeed, must be used alone when filling flexible rubber moulds – but it's worth remembering that candles made from pure paraffin wax burn more quickly than those made with hardener, and they are usually stickier or softer. You can either add hardener, or stearin (stearic acid, see pages 10–11), to paraffin wax yourself, or you can buy pre-mixed paraffin/stearin blends (you can also buy pre-mixed paraffin/beeswax mixtures). It is usual to add up to 10 per cent stearin or stearic acid (see below) when using paraffin wax for candlemaking.

Beeswax, with its warm natural colour and honeyed scent, usually makes a more attractive candle. A natural product of beehives, beeswax can be used by itself. It makes for a hard candle with a long burning time but, just as with paraffin wax candles. If you are using beeswax to make a moulded candle you will need to add a little stearin (not more than 10 per cent) to harden the candles further. Otherwise it is not necessary to use stearin when making beeswax candles. Many church candles are made with a one-in-four proportion of beeswax to paraffin wax. This is because beeswax is considered to be very holy, but because it is more expensive than paraffin wax, churches often decide to use candles made with a mixture of the two waxes. The presence of the paraffin wax also means that the candles will burn more slowly.

Beeswax comes in block form, or it may be bought in sheets, usually about 25 x 40 cm, either solid or honeycombed in pattern, and available in a wide variety of colours, natural and dyed, to make hand-rolled candles. The choice is yours, depending on personal taste and the project involved. It melts at 50–55°C (130–135°F).

As a general rule, use wax with a lower melting point for candles to be made in plastic or rubber moulds and wax with a higher melting point for candles to be made in rigid moulds. This is not, however, an absolute rule.

The important thing to remember about wax – and, indeed, about any aspect of candlemaking – is that WAX IS FLAMMABLE. Never overheat wax, as it can catch fire. Always use a thermometer to monitor the temperature of the wax you are melting when making a project. Don't guess at the temperature to begin with, either, and then insert the thermometer: insert it just as you turn on the heat source, for wax can heat up in seconds. Temperatures are specified for every project in this book. For safety, a double boiler should always be used to melt the wax, so that the melted wax is not directly on the flame. If you don't have a double boiler, you can improvise by placing a bowl into a saucepan filled with water, but I recommend that if you are planning to make candles regularly a double boiler is a good investment.

In case you were wondering, you can also use old store-bought candles to make wax and so make new candles. First scrape away any dirty marks, then simply chop up the candles and scrape away any pieces of wick and charred wick end. This is important, because otherwise the wax will have muddy streaks when re-moulded. Melt coloured waxes separately, otherwise you will end up with a brownish, uninteresting colour. You can also break up old or unwanted candles (store-bought or those you have made yourself) and reuse the pieces in mosaic candles (see pages 46–8). Compared with other crafts, candlemaking is quite economical, since the wax is reusable. The only exception is if wax has been accidentally scorched – then you can't use it again and you will have to dispose of it.

---

*If someone is said to be '**holding a candle to the Devil**' it means they are helping someone who is doing wrong. The saying stems from the Catholic custom of burning candles before the images of saints. To burn a candle before the image of the Devil, and so to honour him, was to be encouraging evil. A similar saying, '**to promise a candle to the Devil**', means that someone is prepared to offer a bribe in order to achieve their aim.*

In the Philippines, a candle dance is danced by girls wishing to attract a lover. This means that a girl can dance with a lighted candle, and then point that candle at a man she likes, without any loss of face or embarrassment.

> # SAFETY NOTES
>
> ❋ If the wax does overheat, **do not attempt to put out the flame with water**. Water will only make the flames spread. Instead, turn off the heat source immediately and smother the flame with the saucepan lid (always keep one close by) or a dampened cloth. This will stop oxygen getting to the wax and so suffocate the flames.
>
> ❋ Other than when a very high temperature is required for a candle, such as the sand candle, **do not burn wax over an open flame.** Use a heat diffuser (heat mat) if you are working on a gas stove.
>
> ❋ When melting wax for candlemaking, **always watch the wax closely and never leave the room.**
>
> ❋ When casting moulds, **do not pour liquid wax anywhere near an open flame.**
>
> ❋ Candlemaking and older children only go together if you supervise the melting of the wax. **Do not melt wax when small children are about, or under foot.** Keep saucepan handles turned away from the edge of the stove.
>
> ❋ With any candles, whether purchased or home-made, **always secure them to a protective base or holder before lighting.** This not only minimises the damage that dripping wax can do to a surface, but is also safer.
>
> ❋ If you wish to dispose of any unwanted wax, pour it into an old tin can or milk carton and put it out for garbage collection. **Never pour melted wax down the sink.**

STEARIN

Stearin, or stearine, or stearic acid, is a fatty acid derived from palm oil. It is added to paraffin wax to harden it. Adding stearin to paraffin wax also makes the finished candle colour more opaque and a richer, though slightly duller, colour than is obtained with just plain wax.

Stearin should be added to paraffin wax and beeswax for all moulded candles, except if the moulds are made of rubber, as the stearin will corrode the rubber over time and so ruin the mould. Stearin comes in small flakes and, occasionally, small tubes that can be shaved off. It is sold in all craft stores that stock candlemaking supplies. In the case of candlemaking kits, such as Candle Magic or

Wizard of the Wick, the stearin is pre-measured and included in the kit.

The stearin is usually added at a rate of 10 per cent of the weight of paraffin wax: for example, 250 g of paraffin wax would require 25 g of stearin. Add the stearin to the double boiler first, and melt it; then add the wax dye if you are using it, then the paraffin wax, and allow them to melt and mix together. The thermometer should be placed in the saucepan when the heat source is turned on.

Stearin may also be used to over-dip a finished candle, to make it harder and give a smooth clear finish. This is not necessary, but it does protect the candles by giving them a smooth skin.

WICKS

If your candles are to burn well they must not only be made of the right sort of wax, but must also have the right kind of wick. Although I show you how to make your own wicks, plain string or twine or plaited cotton is not really satisfactory, and it is quite easy to buy a wide variety of wicks.

Wicking is available in craft shops and through suppliers, and it is quite cheap. It is either round (most suitable for use in beeswax candles and tall, pillar-shaped candles), or flat or semi-flat (suitable for all other types of candles). Most wicking is made up of three main plaited strands, in turn made up of five, eight or even ten threads, depending on the size of the wicking. An efficient wick should curl over as it burns down, which provides a tip that obtains oxygen from the air and so feeds the flame. When setting up to make candles, it's a good idea to buy several different thicknesses of wicking.

Most brands provide an indication of what shape and size candle that particular thickness of wick is suitable for, and a good craft retailer should also be able to give you an indication. As a guide, a 15–ply wick is suitable for candles between 2 and 8 cm in diameter; a thicker, 30–ply wick is needed for very large candles, up to 10 cm in diameter. 'Round' wicking, so named because it is not flat like the plaited wicking, is the best choice for rolled candles like the beeswax candles (see pages 52–4). With a little experimentation, you will soon develop an 'eye' for the right-sized wick for a particular mould or shape. The important thing to remember is that, if the wick is too thick, there will not be enough wax to feed the flame, so the wick will burn on its own, causing the candle to burn too quickly, and sometimes resulting in smoke.

Wicks today are usually made of plaited cotton, and come either 'primed' or 'unprimed'. Primed wicks have simply been pre-treated in wax, which helps the wick to draw up the melted wax to feed the flame, and so reduces the chance of the flame going out. You can prime an unprimed wick by dipping the whole length of wick into plain paraffin wax that has been heated to 70°C (160°F) and leave it there for two to three minutes – and no more. Lift the wick out with a

*'**H**e is not fit to hold a candle to him.' This very old saying dates from the days when young boys were employed to hold candles in theatres and other places of amusement at night time, to light the way for their elders.*

*If a game is **'not worth the candle'**, it means it's not worth the effort. This saying dates from the times when candles were expensive commodities, and it meant that a game, or something similar, wasn't even worth the cost of the candle to light the players.*

skewer or tweezers and, as soon as it can be comfortably handled, run your fingertips *firmly* along the length of the wick to remove excess wax. Dry the wick straight, on greaseproof paper.

I have emphasised that you must apply firm pressure when priming a wick. This helps avoid the problem of a candle 'spitting' when it is lit: spitting is most likely to occur when tiny air pockets trapped around and in the wick have not been filled with wax. As the air in these tiny pockets expands on contact with the candle flame, it bursts through the outer wax film on the wick and spits out a fine spray of wax droplets, which can be dangerous as well as unsightly.

Purchased wicks, whether primed or not, are also usually treated with chemical flame-retardant. Unless you have purchased a pre-packed candlemaking kit, the wicks are usually available wound on cards, or the shop assistant will cut the length you need.

Wicks – unused ones, of course! – can be recycled. If for some reason you're not satisfied with a particular candle project, simply melt it down, hook out the wick with a skewer or fork and set it aside to dry on a piece of greaseproof paper.

If you want to try your hand at making your own wicks from plaited fine string, first make a solution with one cup of water to which you have added two tablespoons of borax and one tablespoon of salt. Immerse the string completely until it is thoroughly saturated. Then hang it up straight to dry. When it is dry, prime it as described above.

Impregnating the wick/string with borax and salt will help to slow down and even out the burning process, so that the string will burn at the correct rate. If the string burns too fast or too slow, it will make the wax melt faster than the flame can consume it, and the candle will drip excessively.

Dyes

Craft shops stock special dyes that are soluble in hot wax. These are available in powder, liquid or granule form or, more usually, in handy wax discs, which are sometimes called 'buds'. With discs, you shave or cut off small pieces of the colour and add to the melted wax or wax-and-stearin mixture to get the colour you want. I like to use the discs, for you can be very precise about adding just the quantity you want to colour the melted wax, and they are less messy and easier to store than powder dyes.

If you are making very large quantities of candles, a usual proportion is around 20 g of dye to every 2 kg of wax. However, you may wish to use less or more; it's entirely up to you. On average, you should calculate that one disc (discs are usually 20 g) will colour 2 kg of wax. Using less colour will create a softer pastel shade, but using a higher ratio is not recommended, as the colour does not always become more intense and can just give a dull sheen to the candle. I have found that it can be necessary to add more dye to beeswax that is a darkish beige or brown colour, to achieve the colour you want. If you want to colour your beeswax candles, I suggest that it is best to buy cream beeswax for the best colour effect.

Dyes come in a wide range of colours. Start with a selection of the primary colours – red, blue and yellow – and the three secondaries – green, orange and purple. You really only need the red, blue and yellow dyes to make any colour you want, and you can experiment with colour combinations and make all the shades of the rainbow by varying quantities. As you gain proficiency, you can experiment with other pre-mixed colours, and black.

The colour of the liquid wax over heat will be very different from the colour it will become when set. While you are waiting for your wax to reach the right temperature, get into the habit of putting a few drops on a piece of greaseproof paper or an old saucer and letting them harden so you can get a more accurate idea of the colour the candle will be when it's hardened.

If you are attempting to make a great many candles all in the same colour, you should try to measure the amount of dye used for each portion of wax carefully, and keep a record of what you did. Also note exactly how much wax and stearin you used, as these can also affect the finished colour intensity. Otherwise, it's almost impossible to duplicate the exact colour.

Scents

If you wish to add perfume to your candles, be sure to use only essential oils or oil blends, or professional candle perfumes available from craft shops. Do not use purchased perfumes or colognes as they contain alcohol and water, and so will not blend properly with wax.

Add perfume towards the end of candlemaking, just as you are about to pour the melted wax into the mould. If it is added at the beginning and so 'cooked' with the wax, the scent may be reduced or changed. There is no need to spend a lot of money on a great many essential oils – a collection of just a few scents, such as rose, pine, lavender and rosemary, will probably be sufficient. The amount of scent used depends largely on your own preference. What may be too subtle for one person's taste may be overpowering to another! I generally find that 8–10 drops of an essential oil will give off a noticeable, but not too dominant, perfume, when the candle is burnt. But do experiment until you find what you like.

Scales and measuring jug

For all the projects described here, I have used ordinary kitchen scales. You can also use a measuring jug to measure the amount of wax for a particular mould. For measuring small amounts, such as stearin, I have used kitchen measures. It is wise to have a separate set for your hobby rather than risk damaging your kitchen set, but I have given some guidance about washing your implements below.

Saucepans and spoons

You will need a double boiler for heating the wax in most of the projects. It makes it easier to control the temperature of the wax. Ideally, the double boiler should be made of stainless steel, which is heavier than aluminium and gives a more even temperature spread.

If you do not have a double boiler, you can easily improvise by placing a heat-proof bowl or saucepan inside another, larger, saucepan containing water. As this can result in uneven temperature, though, you will have to be especially careful when monitoring the temperature of the melting wax. (If you are dipping candles, substitute the bowl with a tall clean dipping can or heat-proof long-sided jug. Professional candlemakers have special dipping cans made of metal, but for home-hobby purposes, you can improvise with a clean empty stainless steel can (see dipping candles, on pages 26–7 for details).

One of the few exceptions to this rule is the sand candle (see pages 24–5). For this project, a wax temperature *higher* than boiling point is required, and the only way to get this is with an open saucepan.

For all your candlemaking requirements, use old saucepans that you no longer wish to use for cooking, or buy inexpensive ones at the supermarket, adding more as you gain in proficiency. As with cooking, a heavy-based saucepan seems to give a better distribution of heat.

When it comes to cleaning your saucepans and other tools, follow these rules:

- Always pour out leftover wax while it's still hot, and store it in an appropriate receptacle.
- Wipe out the saucepan with kitchen paper and then wash it in hot soapy water.
- Use kitchen paper to wipe any chopsticks or old stirring spoons or sticks that you've used to mix the wax and then wash them in hot soapy water. In the case of smaller tools like these, you can also boil them to get rid of any stubborn particles of wax; as the water cools, the wax will solidify and float to the top and can be removed.

Thermometer

For the projects outlined in this book, you will need a confectionery thermometer with a scale between 38°C (100°F) and 110°C (225°F). A candy or cooking thermometer is ideal, and these are available at most craft shops and specialist kitchenware suppliers. Your regular bathroom thermometer is of no use for making candles.

Most candles are made at lower temperatures – dipped candles at 70°C (160°F); rigid mould candles 95°C (200°F); rubber or flexible plastic mould candles 75°C (167°F). The exception is sand candles (see pages 24–5). *Never* attempt candlemaking without a thermometer: it really is critical to success. Too-hot wax can cause patchy or bubbled results; too cool, and you end up with a streaky effect. The newer rigid clear or opaque plastic moulds can tolerate higher temperatures, but the older or flexible ones simply do not, and will buckle or split. Purchased or 'found' metal moulds have the advantage of being able to tolerate very high temperatures, but the sectioned rigid plastic or flexible rubber moulds are easiest for the beginner, so take the time to search out the right sort of thermometer.

WICKING NEEDLES

Most craft shops sell wicking needles. They look like an old-fashioned bodkin or large blunt-ended darning needle and are usually made from stainless steel. Some candlemaking kits have a metal or wooden wicking needle included, which you may reuse. Otherwise, improvise with an old bodkin or skewer or steel knitting needle, depending on the size of the mould. Once the wick is inserted, I have also used old wooden chopsticks and satay sticks many times to secure the end of the wick across the open end of a mould while a candle is cooling.

MOULDS

A wonderful variety of moulds are available in craft shops, made from flexible rubber, rigid treated plastic, either clear or opaque, and, occasionally, glass and metal. They all have a hole for the wick (or are marked in the appropriate spot so you can make the hole, in the case of rubber moulds) and either a rim by which to hang the filled mould in a water bath, or a firm base to stand on as they cool. Commercial candlemakers use moulds made from silicone and metal, which are sometimes copyrighted, but these are not available to the retail shopper, and are extremely expensive.

I have used flexible rubber moulds in the shape of roses and also plain rigid, clear and opaque plastic, oval and square moulds for the candles in this book, for these were the ones most readily available at the time of going to press. Also available are skulls, the three wise monkeys, Buddha figures, stars, Christmas trees, nursery rhyme figures, pine cones, koalas, pyramids, balls, tapers and cats. Fruit, vegetable and flower moulds are readily available outside Australia, and several wholesalers are at present considering introducing these in Australian craft shops. If you are using rubber moulds, or soft formed plastic moulds, the wax temperature should not exceed 75°C (167°F) on your confectionery thermometer.

Simple shapes of rigid plastic moulds, such as the oval and square, snap apart into two pieces. With more complex shapes, there will be more pieces to make removing the finished candle easy. These simple plastic moulds are a good investment for the first-time candlemaker.

Candlewicking is the name given to a type of embroidery with tufts of soft cotton yarn, used mainly to decorate bedspreads and cushions. It is said that snippets of the thick yarn used for the wicks of candles were also put into decorative use on the borders of covers for beds by thrifty housewives in the days of early American settlement, explaining their pretty, classical cream-on-cream appearance.

Actors are a superstitious bunch. A very old belief is that actors don't like to see lighted candles on a stage or in the dressing room because candles indicate there will be a quarrel.

*Opposite: There are many candles that children can enjoy making with their parents.
From top: ice candles (p. 23), shell candles (p. 51), sand candles (p. 24), eggshell candles (p. 42).*

Some are now made with a bump-and-slot arrangement at the sides, so that you have no trouble aligning the two sides correctly; with others, you may have to clamp the two pieces together with either purchased clips or clothes pegs.

When the candle has cooled completely, remove the mould clips or unhinge the moulded snap sections and *very gently* separate the sections of the mould. If you pull too forcefully, you might scratch the candle, or break the mould. If unmoulding is proving difficult, put the mould into the refrigerator for half an hour, then try again.

Candles made in rigid clear or opaque plastic, or in purchased glass or metal moulds, have a slight seam around the middle. To finish, carefully pare this thin ridge of wax back level with the candle face, using a small thin sharp-bladed knife, a Stanley or craft knife, or even a sharpened orange stick. If the mould had a pattern in it, such as curved lines, try to join the lines across the seam by carving with a pointed knife, skewer or orange stick.

With rigid clear or opaque plastic moulds, the wax temperature should not exceed 95°C (200°F). It may even be a lower temperature in the case of some brands – always check the label. (For dipped candles, wax temperature of 70°C (160°F) is correct; the other exception is sand candles, see pages 24–5, where the temperature needs to be much higher, 125°C (260°F).

When it comes to buying candle moulds, the saying that you get what you pay for holds true. I have bought cheap thin plastic moulds and had them buckle and crack after only a single use. It's better to pay the extra for heavy-duty plastic that has been chemically treated to take extreme temperatures. I recommend ArtCrafts rubber moulds, and Candle Magic and WR Design rigid plastic moulds.

Moulds will last much longer if you look after them. Plastic and rubber moulds should be kept in a cool dry place; they must be protected from damp to prevent rotting or slight distortion. Metal moulds should also be kept quite dry to avoid rusting. Wash and dry moulds thoroughly after use, gently clearing away any remaining wax pieces first. With stubborn residual pieces of wax, soak the moulds in warm to hot water, allow the wax to soften, then pick it off before wiping the mould thoroughly. Store moulds with the open end down so that the mould does not get dusty. Before use, wipe out to remove any dust and oil (see page 18).

It's also simple and fun to experiment with making your own moulds, particularly if you're working with children who love the challenge of making things out of 'found objects'. Experimenting with found moulds is also useful when you are starting out and learning about the properties of wax and getting a feel for how candlemaking actually works. As you get better at it, and become more ambitious, you will probably want to invest in purchased professional

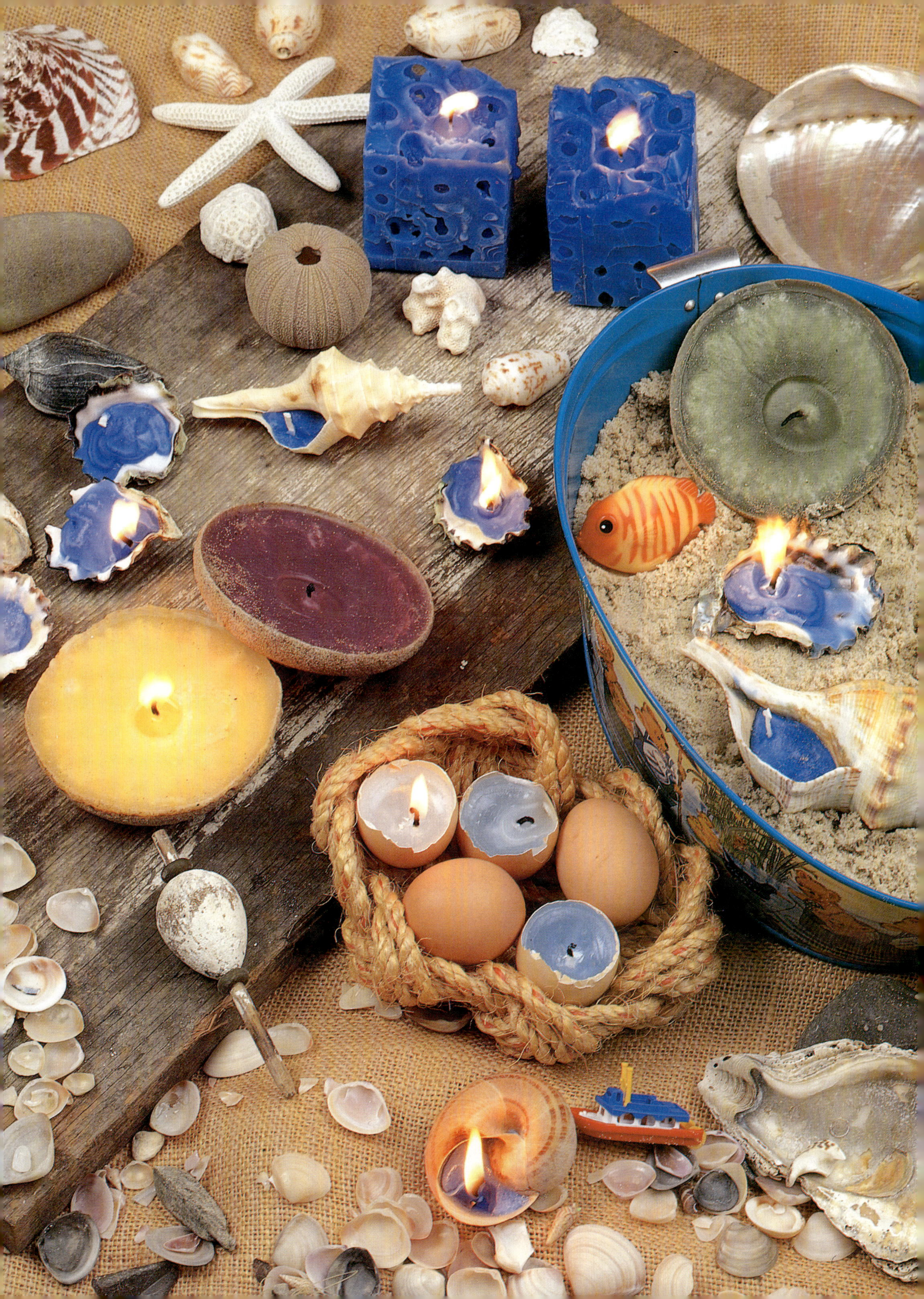

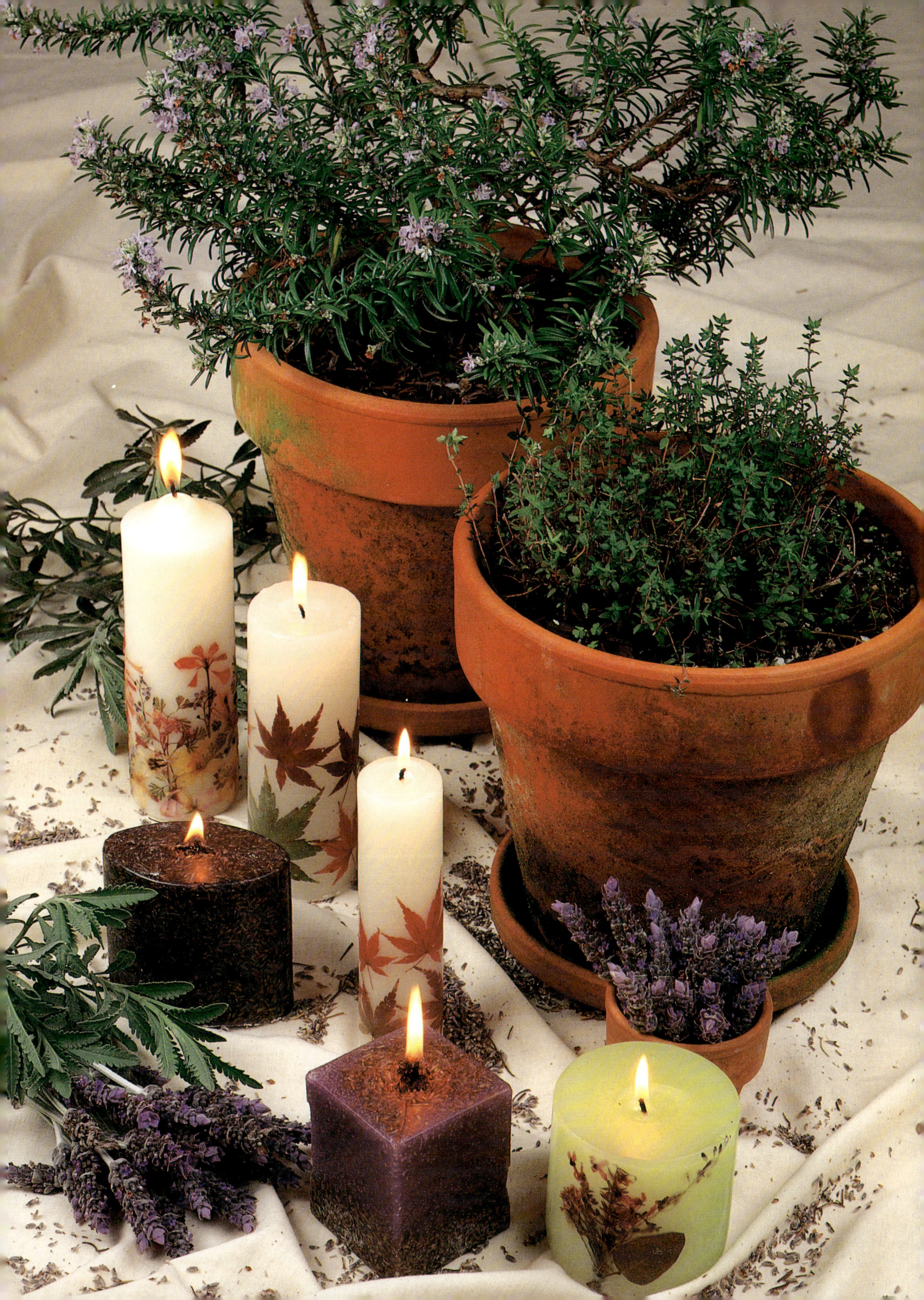

moulds. The only two criteria to be considered with found moulds are that the container you select as a mould should be sturdy enough to withstand the heat of the melted wax, and that you should be able to remove or peel off the mould when the candle has set.

Obviously any mould that has a small top and a large bottom would not be suitable, unless it can be broken or torn away. As a general rule, found or purchased moulds made from glass, metal or plastic give a smooth, shiny finish. Unwaxed cardboard (such as cardboard tubing) gives a rougher, slightly rustic finish which can be very attractive; waxed cardboard (such as in milk cartons) gives an even, slightly matte finish.

All sorts of different household items that might normally be discarded can be recycled as improvised moulds. Cardboard tubes from rolls of cling wrap, paper towelling or toilet paper are usually thick enough to withstand boiling wax, for instance. I've often used cutdown, cleaned milk cartons to make candles, such as the ice candles (see pages 23–4). The cartons are easily obtained and very useful, particularly when you're getting the hang of a technique like making ice candles and you're liable to make mistakes. And you don't have to worry about finicky unmoulding when you're using a milk carton – you just peel and tear it off.

Rigid plastic dishes, tin cans, jars, pottery terrine moulds, wide-necked bottles and ordinary kitchen funnels (with the stem end filled with Blu-tac or mould seal) are just a few other ideas. Funnel-shaped candles make great Christmas trees – simply stud them with gold sequins or tiny pearl beads, or decorate with paint. Small metal patty tins, muffin trays and jelly or pâté moulds make interestingly shaped candles. I used metal patty tins with fluted sides to make the floating candles (pages 31–2), and they make a delightful centrepiece.

With some of these found moulds, such as the tin cans and bottles, you don't have to unmould the candles at all – just leave the wax shape inside for a rustic effect. Two round-bottomed mixing bowls can be used to make a ball candle mould: simply match up the two halves and seal them together, with a length of wick running down the middle, by brushing the two flat faces with a thin coat of wax, then pressing together. Fill and smooth the seam line with a thin sharp knife, camouflaging the line with paint, or other decoration. Eggshells are probably the easiest and most appealing of all found moulds (see pages 42–3).

Another clever idea is to make a decorative finish for a moulded candle using corrugated cardboard. Take a cylindrical mould and a piece of corrugated cardboard. Cut a rectangle from the cardboard, then roll it into a tube shape to fit snugly inside the mould and use masking tape to secure it firmly. Slide the corrugated cardboard inner tube inside the mould, add the wick and fill as you would normally.

Opposite: *You can bring the garden indoors by using pressed flowers or leaves to create individual designs on candles (p.36). Lavender candles (p.39) will perfume your house as they burn.*

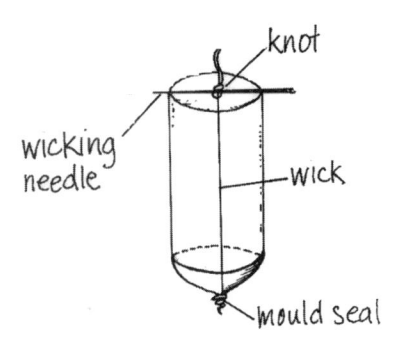

Prepare mould and insert wick.

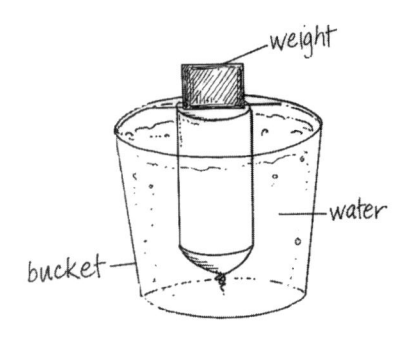

Put weight on top of filled mould in water bath to keep mould stable.

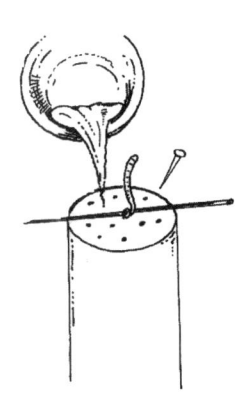

Prick base of candle with a pin and pour in extra hot wax to fill up any indentation caused when the wax contracts. Cool completely before removing candle from mould.

Since you can't oil corrugated cardboard, you will have to tear off the cardboard to unmould the candle; wipe stubborn scraps of cardboard off with a hot wet cloth if necessary.

Before use, prepare the mould by oiling it lightly; take care to remove any heavy streaks or drops of oil as these may leave a mark on the finished surface of the candle. It is easier to unmould wax from an oiled than an unoiled surface. Any light cooking oil is suitable. In some craft shops, you may be able to purchase a silicone aerosol spray. This is an excellent way of preventing rust if you are using a metal purchased or found mould and wish to reuse it. A quick spray of the silicone around the inside of a rigid plastic mould will also help with unmoulding.

If you are using a found mould, especially one made from cardboard like a milk carton or tube, it is a good idea to wrap several lengths of masking tape around the mould horizontally at the top, bottom and in the middle. This will help stop the wax from making the cardboard bulge when you pour it in.

The cooling time for moulded candles is significantly reduced if you use a cold water bath. To make a cold water bath, fill a flat-bottomed bowl or bucket with cold water to a height that will mean that, when you place the mould in it, the water will come up the sides to within 1.5 cm or so of the candle's base. Be very careful not to let any water splash inside the mould or seep in through the wicking hole. Stand the candle mould in the water bath and place a weight on top of it to keep it quite straight and stop it from bobbing around. (The weight could be an old half-brick, a full food tin, clean empty terracotta flower pots or wood chocks. Don't use books!)

> **Note** When making any kind of moulded candle, whether it's the sand candle or a candle using a purchased rigid mould, it's important that you watch it closely as it cools. This is because, as the wax temperature cools and the candle solidifies, it will shrink slightly and, depending on the size and shape of the candle mould, you will end up with either a dip in the middle or a hollowed-out centre at the base, which is both unstable and unattractive. The solution is to always keep a little extra wax in the same colour, heat it to the same temperature as described in the candlemaking instructions for moulding the candle, and use it to top up the shrunken area.

Mould seal

You need mould seal, a putty-like substance available from craft shops, to secure the top end of the wick where it protrudes from a mould while it is being cooled in a water bath, and so prevent water leaking into the mould and ruining your candle. Be generous with your mould seal – even a single drop of water getting inside the mould will result in an ugly mark on the finished candle.

Mould seal also has a number of other uses – from firming a stubborn wick end around a wicking needle, to holding a candle base steady while you make an ice candle (see pages 23–4. Reuse by picking off cooled wax scraps and pressing them together. Improvise with Blu-tac or Plasticine, if no mould seal is available.

OTHER EQUIPMENT

It's a good idea to collect the following articles and keep them in your craft box or drawer along with other candlemaking equipment:

- Kitchen skewers, metal knitting needles, bodkins, etc.
- Wire
- Orange sticks or thin dowelling, or old wooden (not plastic) chopsticks to use in place of wicking needles
- Lipped ladles, for neatly pouring wax into tiny moulds
- An old tea pot or spouted watering can, which can be useful for pouring liquid wax into moulds in a slow, thin stream, and so help eliminate bubbles
- Flexible oven mitts
- Sharp palette knife or old paring knife, for skimming off uneven edges on moulded candles
- Old baking dish or plates, for placing shells or floating candle moulds on before filling
- Masking tape, for holding wicks in place in purchased moulds
- Scissors, for cutting wicks
- Pencil and paper, for making notes
- Greaseproof paper, for drying wicks on
- Pillow case and hammer, for breaking up old chunks of wax or purchased candles to re-melt or make a mosaic candle (see pages 46–8)
- Newspaper
- Old pantyhose or polishing cloth.

TOP TIPS FOR A PROFESSIONAL FINISH

- Best results are usually achieved when you work in a room with a warm, even temperature, rather than one that is too cold or overheated, both of which will interfere with the heating and cooling stages of the wax.

- Moulded candles can be cooled at room temperature, but best results will be achieved if you cool them in a cold water bath (see page 18 for details). This makes for a smoother, more satiny finish to your candle, whereas ones cooled at room temperature look more

The first anti-superstition group, which went under the impressive name of the National Committee of Thirteen against Superstition, has met regularly on unlucky Fridays in the USA since the 1940s. At meetings, held at tables under open umbrellas, a cake set with thirteen lighted candles would be served.

FAMOUS WORDS ABOUT CANDLES

Light another's candle, but don't put out your own.
Traditional

How inferior for seeing with, is your brightest train of fireworks to the humblest farthing candle!
Carlyle, *Essays: Diderot*

Then he never snuffed a candle with his fingers.
Charles I of Spain, reading upon the tombstone of a Spanish nobleman, 'Here lies one who never knew fear.' (Boswell, Johnson, 1769)

The smallest candle fills a mile with its rays, and the papillae of man run out to every star.
Emerson, *Conduct of Life: Fate*

*My candle burns at both ends;
It will not last the night;
But ah, my foes and oh, my friends –
It gives a lovely light!*
Edna St Vincent Millay,
A Few Figs from Thistles: First Fig

*Saith Nature thus gave her the praise,
To be the chiefest work she wrought,
In faith, methink, some better ways
On your behalf, might well be sought,
Than to compare, as ye have done,
To match the candle with the sun.*
Henry Howard,
Sonnet to the Fair Geraldine

*She would rather light a candle than curse the darkness
and her glow has warmed the world.*
Adlai E. Stevenson, Tribute to Eleanor Roosevelt on her death. (This is now used as a motto by the Eleanor Roosevelt Memorial Foundation.)

amateurish. If you're in a real hurry, you can cool a candle down in the refrigerator, but this is not really recommended for general cooling, as the humidity can alter the appearance of the candle as it cools. (You can, however, place a hardened candle that is proving stubborn to unmould in the refrigerator for half an hour, with good results.)

- When pouring hot wax into a mould, pour evenly and slowly to help prevent air bubbles getting trapped in the wax. Always fill a mould completely so that the shape will be even and smooth when unmoulded. Don't fill the mould half way, allow it to cool and then add more, unless, of course, a deliberate colour contrast is being sought.

- Making a deliberate colour contrast is the way to make a layered or a rainbow candle. Fill the mould with the first colour to the desired level of stripe, say, 3 cm. Allow it to cool and top up the depression with extra heated wax. When the first colour has hardened completely, use a skewer to poke a few holes on the base of the first colour stripe. Then heat the wax for the second layer and pour it over the top of the first, again filling up the side of the mould to a predetermined level. The second colour will fill in where you have made holes, forming a snug locking device. Candles made up of layers of wax like this tend to be a little fragile. To make them more secure, dip the whole, cooled candle in a dipping tin filled with clear hot wax or wax that has been tinted in a complementary shade. This will form a wall around the candle and keep the discs in place.

- It is important, where possible, to warm the mould first, and to work quickly to fill the warmed mould with hot wax before the mould cools. You obviously can't do this with all moulds, such as cardboard ones, but it's easy with rigid plastic ones: soak them in a sink full of hot water for a few minutes before drying and oiling lightly, then fill. Not only will they fit together better if they are sectioned moulds, but warming the moulds minimises the tiny surface bubbles that you are likely to get when you pour hot wax into cold moulds. With metal and glass moulds, it is possible to warm them for a few minutes in a slow oven – no more than 80°C (180°F).

- Once you've poured the hot wax in, tap the sides of the mould gently with your fingernails. This will help any trapped air bubbles rise to the surface, which can be a particular problem with moulds that have uneven edges, such as roses and pine cones. Be gentle! Even a tiny dent in a mould can spoil the finished candle's appearance, as well as making it difficult to unmould. This is particularly important with glass moulds, which can shatter if tapped with a metal rod or pencil while they are filled with hot wax, and for purchased rigid moulds, which can blow out at a point weakened by being tapped with a hard object.

- With moulded candles, you will find that, as the wax begins to cool, a small depression forms in the centre of the candle. Always keep a little bit of wax back from the initial amount poured into the mould, and then heat it to the same temperature as before and pour in and to fill the depression. Depending on the size of the candle (and therefore, how long it will take to cool completely), you may need to repeat this step several times.

- Another good tip to remember, particularly with large or thick moulded candles: as the wax cools and hardens and a depression forms in the base (as described above), take a piece of very fine wire and pierce several holes down through its base towards the top, about half way between the side and the centre. This helps any trapped air bubbles to escape and makes for a candle that burns more evenly. Then pour over the reserved heated wax to fill in the depression.

- Keep your equipment clean. Scrape up left-over wax pieces and either collect them for a mosaic candle project (see pages 46–8), or remelt them for another project.

- Always spread plenty of newspaper over the workspace you intend to use for making candles, including the floor.

- When making moulded candles, hang the mould over the neck of a wide-mouthed jug or old bowl, or stand it in an old baking tray so that any seepage from the wick end will be contained and not mark a table or floor. Placing about 5 mm of water at the bottom of the jug or tray will mean that, if some wax does drip out, it will not adhere to the tray but can easily be lifted out of the water.

- If you *do* get hot wax splashes on a stove or in the sink, scrape them up when cool and, if the surface allows, wipe over with methylated spirits.

- Always leave moulded candles to cool completely – for at least 8 to 10 hours, but preferably overnight. If the mould is a rigid one (and it was properly oiled and prepared) a gentle tug on the wick from the bottom should make the candle start to slide out. Candles that have been moulded in rubber may need a little more elbow grease to gently roll and smooth the mould back on itself in order to unmould the candle. If a candle is proving particularly stubborn, put it in the refrigerator for half an hour before attempting to unmould it again.

Be of good comfort, Master Ridley, and play the man.
We shall this day light such a candle, by God's grace, in England,
as I trust shall never be put out.
Hugh Latimer, at the stake of Nicholas Ridley, who was burned with him for heresy, 16 October 1555

It is better to light one candle than to curse at the darkness.
Author unknown

To enlarge or illustrate the power and effect of love
is to set a candle in the sun.
Robert Burton,
The Anatomy of Melancholy, pt 3

The artificial production and supply of light during the absence of the sun, unquestionably holds a distinguished rank among the most important arts of civilised life.
Frederick Accum, 1815

Neither do men light a candle, and put it under a bushel, but on a candlestick, and it giveth light to all that are in the house.
New Testament: Matthew v.15

I'll be a candle-holder, and look on ...
Wm. Shakespeare, Romeo And Juliet, Act I, sc. 4, l 38.

And then, exulting in their taper, cry
'Behold the sun!' and Indian-like, adore!
Young, Night Thoughts, Night iv, l. 779.

As a white candle
In a holy place
So is the beauty
Of an aged face
Joseph Campbell, (Irish poet 1879-1944), The Old Woman

- For all the candles you make, whether they're moulded or dipped, pay particular attention to finishing off the bottom, otherwise the candles will have a lean to them. The bottom edges are usually uneven and, in the case of moulded candles, can be quite sharp. Trim the bottom edge of the candle carefully with a thin sharp knife. Use smooth, shaving motions rather than trying to saw, as the wax can break off raggedly, leaving you worse off than before. After scraping the wax to a level finish, smooth it by standing it on a hot plate or even sliding it up and down an old hot iron.

- To give your candles a professional smooth gleaming finish, buff the surface with a wadded-up old nylon pantyhose leg that has been dipped lightly in unscented vegetable oil (not olive oil – it leaves a cloudy look). Using a purchased polishing cloth – one of the ones that's been impregnated with beeswax – is also a great way of smoothing out any tiny imperfections in a finished candle and giving it a satiny look.

- When storing your candles, make sure you choose a cool place where there is little or no dust. A wardrobe or drawer is better than a kitchen cupboard or laundry shelf. Wrap each candle in tissue, greaseproof paper or cling wrap to prevent marks on its surface. Do not wrap candles in newspaper, as the print will mark the sides of the candle. Keep candles well away from any sources of heat, such as fires, radiators, clothes driers, the sun, hot water pipes or stoves.

Candles to Make

ICE CANDLE

IF YOU HAVE A CHILD who is becoming interested in natural science and how things work, this is a good project to do together. With an ice candle, the ice hardens the hot wax on contact, before it has time to melt the ice; the ice then melts, leaving interesting-shaped holes in the wax. I've used a milk carton, but you can use a round mould or cylindrical mould. If you do use a mould, instead of using a wick, simply run a narrow (about 1 cm) candle through the wicking hole, and cut it to the same length as the mould.

YOU WILL NEED

Milk carton
Small (20–25 cm) candle or taper, about 1 cm in diameter
200 g paraffin wax
10 g stearin
1 wax dye disc
Small ice cubes (about 1 cm), or ice cubes crushed to this size
Double boiler
Old spoon or stirring stick
Wax thermometer

The above quantities will make approximately 2 candles.

METHOD

Wash and dry the milk carton thoroughly. Cut down the sides until you have a box about 20 cm high. Oil the inside of the carton very lightly with plain vegetable oil, being careful not to leave an excess.

Place the stearin and wax thermometer into a double boiler or in an old tin can standing in a saucepan of simmering water, and melt. Add a few shavings of the wax dye disc. Add the paraffin wax and melt, adding further shavings from the disc until you have the colour you want, and stirring all the while with an old spoon or stirring stick. Monitor temperature carefully until it is 80°C (176 °F).

Stand the small candle in the centre of the carton and see how high it reaches – if it protrudes past the top of the carton, trim 1 cm or so off its base. Then pour a little of the melted coloured wax into the base of the milk carton and when it has hardened slightly, stand the small candle in the melted wax until it has set enough to stand alone.

TIP
A spray of cooking oil is sufficient to oil a mould, and will mean that the candle will unmould more easily when it has cooled.

TIP
To gauge the colour of the finished candle, simply remove a little of the coloured wax as it is being heated and place it in a small bowl of cold water so it sets. You will be able to see whether it is intense enough.

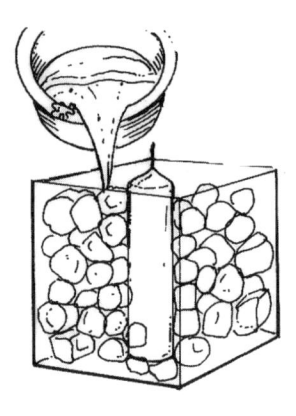

Fill mould with chunks of ice and cover with hot wax.

NOTE
Unlike the other candles described in this book, the wax needs to be heated to a higher temperature when making sand candles – the hotter the wax, the more wax will seep into the sand, making a firm outer crust for the finished candle, rather than a patchy effect. For this reason an open saucepan is used rather than a double boiler, because in the latter the wax will not go above the temperature of boiling water. Do be careful and use your wax thermometer to monitor the temperature of the candle wax constantly, for wax heated to high temperatures is, naturally, a fire risk. It is just as volatile as hot cooking oil. Keep a saucepan lid at hand to smother any flames.

Check that the wax is still at 80°C (176 °F). It is important that the temperature stays at 80°C, so you may need to reheat the wax before continuing. Quickly fill the carton with small ice cubes or broken large ice cubes – trying not to shift the small standing candle. (The size of the ice cubes is critical to the success of this candle, and you may need to make a couple of attempts to get the result you're looking for. Too-small ice pieces will melt too quickly, while too-large ones will leave uneven spaces.) If you have to wait while wax is heating, or reheating, pour any melted water out of the carton.

Swiftly, and with one smooth quick movement, pour the hot wax over the carton filled with broken ice so that the melted wax reaches right up to the top of the inserted candle. Again, this step requires a bit of practice to get right – if you pour too fast you will trap air; if you pour too slowly, you will melt the ice unevenly. Be sure to keep the central candle straight as the wax hardens around it. Leave the candle to cool and harden completely at room temperature.

When the candle has cooled, cut and peel away the milk carton surrounds and dry the candle thoroughly. Buff the outer surface of the candle with a soft cloth dipped in vegetable oil. You may want to run a sharp, thin-bladed knife down the four corners of the candle as the edges can be quite sharp.

Shake the candle and, if you can hear water sloshing around inside, pierce the bubble(s) with a pin to let the water out.

SAND CANDLE

Sand candles are made, quite simply, by creating an impression in damp sand and filling it with wax. These really are so simple to make, that even a child can create a sand candle. (Obviously, though, adult supervision is required with the heating of the wax.)

There's also something very satisfying about working with basic, natural materials – in this case, just coloured wax and clean sand. You can obtain a lovely, glowing candle that looks particularly lovely outdoors, without having to spend a cent on moulds or decorative finishes.

I used sand purloined from my children's sand pit for this candle. You can, of course, have a lot of fun experimenting with different colours and grades of sand – you can even buy silver sand or coloured sand from some hardware shops.

YOU WILL NEED
Slightly dampened sand
Large mixing bowl
Smaller round bowl or simply shaped, flat-bottomed jelly mould, such as a star or oval
Appropriate length of wicking
Wicking needle

500 g paraffin wax
25 g stearin
1 wax dye disc
Double boiler
Old spoon or stirring stick
Wax thermometer

The above quantities will make approximately 4 candles.

METHOD

Prime the wick and set it aside (see Getting Started, pages 11–12). Place the slightly dampened sand in a large mixing bowl so that it is about half full. Press down the smaller mixing bowl or jelly mould in the centre, packing the sand firmly in around the mould or bowl. It is important to press the sand in and around the mould or bowl *very* evenly and smoothly, as this will ensure an even finish to the candle. Carefully remove the mould or bowl, lifting it straight up so no sand is knocked back into the impression. If this does happen, simply start over and make another impression.

Heat the stearin in an old saucepan and add shavings from the dye disc until you have the colour you want. Add the paraffin wax and continue to heat gently until you reach 125°C (260°F).

Gently pour about half of the hot wax into the impression left by the mould. Try to pour evenly and avoid dislodging any of the sand with the wax as it goes in, so that the impression holds its shape. A good method is to pour the hot wax over the back of an old spoon, as this helps to disperse the wax evenly and softly, rather than pouring a thin stream of wax into the impression, which can create uneven holes.

Wait for a few minutes, during which time quite a lot of the wax will have seeped into the walls of the impression, and so have begun to create the crust. Reheat the remaining wax again to 125°C (260°F) and continue filling the mould, retaining a little bit of wax to fill the depression that will form as the candle cools.

Set the bowl aside and allow the wax to cool. After about two hours, a well will form in the centre of the candle. Push the wicking needle down through the middle of the softened wax and press in an appropriate length of wicking, leaving about 2.5 cm protruding from the top of the candle. Wind the excess wick around the wicking needle and lay it across the top of the candle. Heat the remaining wax and use it to top up the candle around the depression. Set the sand candle aside and leave it to cool completely for seven to eight hours, or overnight.

The next day, slide your hands under the sand candle and remove it. Discard the sand or keep it for another project. If you want a smooth finish on the candle, use a rasp to buff it gently and get rid of any lumps and bumps. Smooth the base so that the candle will stand steady, and trim the wick.

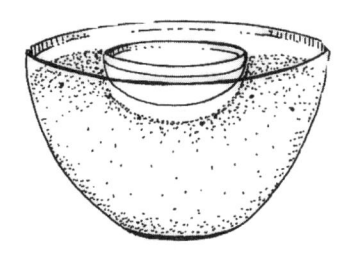

Push small bowl into damp sand to form an indentation.

SAFETY CAUTION
Do not leave heating wax unattended, as it is a fire hazard at such high temperatures.

*Tapers originated in France in the middle of the seventeenth century; they were called **bougies** and were made from beeswax. Tapers were used mainly to melt sealing wax used for envelopes, as well as to light lamps.*

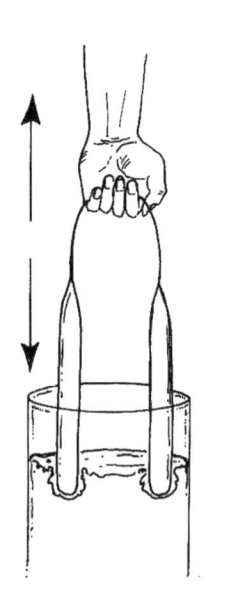

Hold wick with spread fingers so that the two candles won't touch.

Dipped Candle

Dipping is probably the oldest way of making candles – it is also one of the simplest, although it does take a little more time. The process is, simply, one of dipping a pair of wicks or a single wick into a large deep can of liquid wax, leaving the wax to dry for a few seconds, then repeating until you have built up a thick coating of wax in a tapered shape. Every time you dip the wicks you build up the shape and thickness of the candles. As you become more proficient, you can make them taper towards the tip. Hand-dipped candles are very slim and elegant.

You will need

1 long straight-sided dipping can or heat-proof jug, about 25 cm high and 13 cm in diameter
Lengths of wick: about 60 cm for each pair of 25 cm candles
2 kg paraffin wax
1 wax dye disc
8–10 drops of essential oil or oil blend combination
Double boiler
Old spoon or stirring stick
Wax thermometer

The above quantities will make approximately 12 candles, depending on their thickness.

Method

Prime the wick(s) and set aside (see Getting Started, pages 11–12). Put the paraffin wax into the dipping can and stand the can in a saucepan; fill the saucepan with enough water to reach about halfway up the sides of the dipping can. Place over heat, insert the wax thermometer, and bring to a simmer. Stir the wax occasionally as it melts. When the temperature reaches 70°C (160°F), you are ready to start.

To colour the wax, add shavings of wax dye disc, stirring well with a stirring stick or old spoon to combine. Add 8–10 drops of essential oil or oil blend, if desired. Check that the temperature has not dropped. Fold the wick in half and hold the centre of the wick over your fingers so that two strands of wick are kept separate. Dip the wick ends into the melted wax to a depth of about 23–25 cm (will depend on height of can) and leave for a minute. Lift the 'candles' straight up and out, in a smooth motion. Have something nearby to hook the dipped candles over as they cool between dips – a drying rack or broom handle could be rigged up to serve this purpose. Leave them to dry for approximately three minutes. The wax will only drip if you have let the candles dip for too long.

Dip again, this time for a count of three. Continue dipping for three second intervals, and removing to cool for about three minutes between dips, then dipping again. Continue for about fifteen to twenty dips, or until the candles are the thickness you want. Check the temperature constantly – if the wax becomes too cool, then you will get lumps on the sides of the dipped candles; if the temperature is too hot, it will melt the previous layers and result in uneven sides.

To give the candles a smooth, professional finish, heat the remaining wax to 85°C (180°F) then dip the pair(s) of candles into the wax for the count of three. Leave them to cool for one minute, then dip for another count of three, then hang up to cool and harden completely. While the candles are still soft, even out the wick ends by smoothing them gently with your forefinger and thumb, and trim the bases with a sharp knife so they are neat and flat.

When you are comfortable with the dipping technique, you may wish to make more than one pair of dipped candles at the one time. However, it is probably easier at the start to make one pair at a time.

Variation Instead of using plain coloured wax, experiment with creating a shaded effect on your dipped candles. This is achieved by dipping the candles in plain white wax, right up until the last three or four dips. At this stage, while the candles are hanging up and cooling, add shavings from a dye disc and mix well. Check the temperature, then dip the candles at varying depths into the newly coloured wax, to get a gradation of tone.

TIP
When making your first dipped candles, it's inevitable that you'll end up with a few that are bent! But it's easy to straighten them again. Simply dip the hardened candle into an upright container of warm (not boiling hot) water and leave for five to ten minutes. A lot will depend on the thickness of the candle, so use common sense and your fingers to tell you when the candle is becoming pliable again. Lift the warm candle out of the water and roll it to and fro on a cold hard surface, such as a Laminex bench top or a marble pastry slab. Repeat if necessary.

DIPPED AND MOULDED

In early times candlemaking was a slow and laborious business: the first stage was the preparation of the wicks, which were usually made from cotton, wound together and cut to the lengths required. As with candle making today, it was an art to both cut the wick at a slight angle so the candle would burn without spluttering, and also to ensure the wick was absolutely straight and free from knots, so that the candle would burn evenly.

Candles were then dipped in a dipping frame – a large wooden frame from which the wicks were suspended – and dipped into a large cauldron filled with melted tallow (animal fat). Since tallow candles went rancid if they were exposed to the air for too long, they were often stored in barrels of bran or, in wealthier households, special airtight tinplate candle boxes. These boxes were often beautifully decorated and embossed with the household insignia or crest, and many may be seen today in museums around the world. In poorer households, salt boxes and candle boxes were usually both made of hard wood, and, again, carved and decorated in a similar way. The hinged salt box was kept near the fire while the candle box was stored in an upright position, away from the heat. Often these boxes were handed down from generation to generation, or were made and given as wedding presents.

Candles play a part in many old rituals to do with love and courtship. If a girl wishes to see a lover who is far away she should, according to English superstition, put two pins in a lighted candle and recite this poem:

'Tis not these pins I wish to burn,
But ...'s heart I wish to turn.
May he neither sleep nor rest
'Til he has granted my request.

By the time the candle had burned down to the pins, the fellow was supposed to be by her side. A similar ritual and rhyme could be used to bring a love affair to an end.

As time passed, moulded candles became considered superior to dipped candles. These were developed in France during the fifteenth century AD. Moulds produced candles that had a more even, smooth finish than was possible for a dipped candle. They were also usually made with better quality tallow which had been processed to remove impurities, thus it was less smelly and whiter. These tallow candles were favoured for ceremonial use and for use in grand homes, which might otherwise have only used beeswax candles. The wicks of moulded candles were usually dipped in beeswax as an additional refinement, too. Later improvements saw wicks being plaited and pickled or soaked in various solutions, commonly boracic acid, to help slow down combustion and prevent the production of ash.

Interestingly, the craftsmen who made candle moulds were usually pewterers too, and many were acclaimed for designing beautiful candlesticks and candle holders for noble families. In New York, in 1784, a Mr Cornelius Bradford and a Mr Malcom M'Euen, lumberers and pewterers, advertised that, for tallow chandlers and spermaceti works, they make the best double polished candle moulds for all sizes. Such moulds were described clearly in 1855:

The moulds used in making candles are of pewter, and consist of two parts; namely, a hollow cylinder of the length of the candle open at both ends, and nicely polished on the inside; and a small metallic conical cap with a hole in the centre for the wick.

Today, of course, the sort of moulds you can buy to experiment with candlemaking at home are usually made from heatproof formed synthetic material, either rigid or rubbery in texture, depending upon the style. Moulds are also made from metal and treated glass, or you can improvise with found moulds, using almost any heatproof material, such as the milk cartons and shells used in this book.

TWISTED CANDLE

Did you enjoy playing with clay and Plasticine when you were a child? I did! And making twisted candles will be child's play for anyone who likes to make things. The procedure is very straightforward – all you need to do is to flatten a still-warm dipped candle, then gently and evenly twist it. Long tapers will look very elegant, but it's also fun to use this technique on short dipped candles, too, and so make quaint little curly twisted candles. As with most of the projects described here, practice will produce near-perfect results, but it doesn't really matter if you don't manage to twist the candle evenly – after all, you are producing a unique, hand-made item, and any seeming flaws only emphasise the fact that you've made it yourself!

You will need

2 (or more) warm, newly dipped candles (see previous instructions)
Wooden rolling pin

Method

Place the warm candle on a clean firm surface: a marble pastry slab is ideal, but any bench surface or table top will do. But remember, you will have to clean the wax off.

Leaving about 2.5 cm at the bottom of the candle in a roundish shape (so it will still fit into a candle holder), gently and evenly flatten the rest of the candle with the rolling pin until it is about 5 mm thick. Hold the base of the candle still with your left hand and hold the wick end between the thumb and forefinger of your right hand. Keeping the base end still, start twisting the candle with your other hand; try to get the twist starting near the bottom of the candle and work towards the tip for best results. If you want only a slightly curved, flared look, then just turn and twist the softened candle once or twice, turning it steadily as you do. Repeat the process if you want a more exaggerated twist.

Whatever effect you want, you will need to be gentle and consistent – if you apply too much uneven pressure to the wax it may break. You will also need to work quite swiftly so that the wax stays soft enough to twist, but the whole process should take no more than a minute or so. Set the candle aside to cool and harden for at least one hour.

Variation If you do not have any newly made dipped candles handy, it is still possible to make twisted candles. Take cold firm candles, ones you have made or bought, and dip them in a can of heated wax, coloured to match or to contrast with the existing candle, and soften them this way before rolling and twisting, as above. Most candles will be soft enough to twist after about one minute in the hot wax.

Painted Candles

If you are artistic, the sky's the limit with painted candles! It's quick, easy and fun to take a plain cream or white purchased candle and paint it with flowers, scenes and decorations. You can buy or make small egg-shaped candles and paint on a spray of lily of the valley, a daffodil or a bunch of violets.

And even if you're not confident about drawing and painting freehand onto a candle, I'm sure you can manage dots and squiggles in gold, or even just plain bands of colour. Several shades of the same colour can be used for an interesting layered look, or different colours can be used to make a rainbow effect. Or paint criss-cross lines of

Flatten out dipped candle with a rolling pin.

Hold bottom of flattened candle with your left hand and twist gently with your right hand.

Tip

Even the most experienced candlemakers end up with a few breakages sometimes. If you've twisted your dipped candle too enthusiastically and it has broken, don't despair – it's still possible to fix it. Melt a little wax in the same colour and brush the broken ends before pressing them firmly together. You could also improvise by covering the mark with strips of appliquéd wax, perhaps in a bow shape, or with a thin line of gold sealing wax.

colour to produce a charming country 'gingham' look. Themes provide inspiration, too – what about painting on silver or gold numerals and then sprinkling with gold or silver glitter for an anniversary table decoration? Another good idea is to make or buy moulded candles that have raised or carved portions, and then highlight these features with paint. You are limited only by your imagination, and the time and patience needed to practise this craft.

When it comes to selecting paints for decorating candles, special candle paints are available, but you can also use poster paints or even oil paints. Provided the painting is relatively light, neither should interfere with burning, but a solid coating of acrylic, oil or poster paint would interfere with the smooth burning of the candle, so use common sense.

Another idea is to melt down broken crayons, and then keep the resulting wax liquid by putting the colours on an old saucer or saucepan lid over a saucepan of simmering water. You can also use up scrapings of coloured candle wax in this way. I have used poster paints here because I find the colours more appealing. It's important, though, to check with your supplier whether the paint you select will give off toxic fumes when heated – most manufacturers advise on the back of the pack whether this is the case. You can easily experiment with candles that have, say, the same basic colour but are different heights or shapes.

Practise your design on a piece of scrap paper first. Once you have painted a candle, whether it's with paint or wax, you can't remove the marks. If your design is a naive, folk-art style, then the odd unplanned splash just adds to the charm, so beginners may find it best to use these styles, rather than very formal or detailed ideas. I also like the effect of just running squiggly gold lines and curlicues around a candle – awfully easy and very quick. If you feel ambitious, then try your hand at flowers or even a scene if the candle shape suggests this to you.

YOU WILL NEED

A selection of plain white or cream candles
Poster paints
A fine paintbrush

METHOD

Wipe the candles clean with a damp cloth and leave them to air-dry completely, so that you will be working on a surface that is free of dust or grease. Practise your design on a piece of scrap paper. To give yourself confidence, particularly if you're painting lines or horizontal patterns, you could use a pin to make very light marks on the candle to help guide you in placing the paint.

Place the candle flat on your work surface. Paint on the design slowly and carefully, and leave the paint to dry before rolling the candle around to work on the opposite side. Let the candle dry thoroughly before lighting it.

Variation Use a pin or darning needle to prick or carve out a pattern on the candle before painting to create a textured effect. Sharp-bladed thin knives, orange sticks and toothpicks are all useful carving tools if you want to accentuate your design. One idea that is easy to copy is a birth candle. Take a thick candle and carve the new baby's name or initials on it and date of birth on it, then paint or sponge-paint over whole candle with pink or blue. Pick out initials and numbers with gold paint if you like, then buff the candle for extra lustre and to soften the edges of the carved letters.

FLOATING CANDLES

There's something very romantic and exotic about a bowl filled with floating candles. Choose a bowl that's large enough to float a few luscious-looking perfumed flowers as well, such as jasmine, camellias or rose petals, or even just tiny florets from a hydrangea. Floating candles make an extremely beautiful centrepiece for a party.

Some craft suppliers keep professional moulds that turn out rose- or lily-shaped floating candles, but you may have to put in some research to find them. Using small decorative jelly moulds or tins, as I have used here, is a far easier option.

YOU WILL NEED

6 small jelly moulds or cake tins with fluted sides
Lengths of wick
Mould seal or Plasticine
250 g paraffin wax
25 g stearin
1 wax dye disc
Double boiler
Old spoon or stirring stick
Wax thermometer

METHOD

Prime the wicks and set them aside (see Getting Started, pages 11–12).

Wipe out the tins or moulds with a very little vegetable oil to facilitate removal of the moulded candle when it has cooled and hardened. Place the moulds on a flat, level surface, securing each one with a blob of mould seal or Plasticine on its underside to keep it level if it has a curved base.

Place stearin in the double boiler and melt. Add shavings of the dye disc until the desired colour intensity is reached, stirring all the time with an old spoon or stirring stick. Add the paraffin wax and

---

In the days before electricity, a flickering candle was thought to signal that death was near, even if no one in the house was ill at the time. Similarly, if the candle burned unevenly and wax collected down one side in a so-called 'winding sheet' or shroud shape, this was a very bad omen, too.

TIP
Always look for moulds that are wider around the top than at the bottom, otherwise the candles will not unmould.

Tip
Depending on how firm or soft the wax is – which will depend on such things as the size of the mould or how hot or cold the room is – you may have to help things along by starting the wick hole off first with a wooden toothpick, or, if the wax is still very soft, holding the wicks upright for a minute or two until they're firm enough to leave.

Opposite: Dipped (p.26) and twisted (p. 28) candles make elegant mantelpiece or table settings.

Inside left: By using rubber moulds and leftover pieces of wax you can create some stunning candles: mosaic candles (p. 46), rose candles (p. 34), medieval candle (p. 48).

continue to heat. Use a wax thermometer to check when the temperature reaches 85°C (180°F).

Pour the melted wax into the tins or moulds, but leave a little space at the top. Allow to stand for a minute, then gently tap the sides of the mould with a knife handle to bring any air bubbles to the top. Leave to cool and harden slightly.

As the candles cool, they will shrink away from the edges a little, and a shallow well will form in the centre. At this stage, reheat the remaining wax to 85°C (180°F) and pour it into the centre of each candle. While the centres of the candles remain soft, snip pieces of wick to lengths that will protrude about 2.5 cm from the top of the candle, and push them into wax while it is still softened.

When the candles are quite hard, trim the wicks to about 1 cm from the top of the candle and turn them out of the moulds.

Variation Small embossed or patterned jelly moulds make interesting floating candles. Heart, fish and star shapes are readily available. Fill these shapes to a depth of only about 2.5 cm and then float the completed candles in a bowl of water for a delightful centrepiece.

Idea If you want to make a lot of larger floating candles, say, for use in a swimming pool at a party, here is a cheat's method for making wicks the easy way. Cut small birthday candles to the right height for your mould. Melt the wax at the base of the candle and hold it upright in the centre of the mould until it is firm, then fill the mould with melted wax to wick height.

SNUFFED OUT

When houses were lit entirely by candles, snuffers – usually of polished steel – and douters were just as important as candle holders in all their variety. Snuffers were a sort of scissor, which were used to trim the wick so the candle burnt straight and did not gutter. Wicks were a constant source of trouble. If, in the course of burning, they were not completely consumed and charred, bits accumulated and ran down the side of the candle. This meant that the charred ends of the wicks also had to be constantly snipped off while the candle burned so that they did not dip down into the melted wax and go out.

In large houses, where all the candles were lit, the job of keeping them all 'snuffed' could keep several servants fully occupied all evening! Snuffing was thought to be necessary at half-hourly intervals during burning – not only was an unsnuffed candle wasteful of its own substance, but also it gave only a fraction of the light of a properly cared-for one. This was

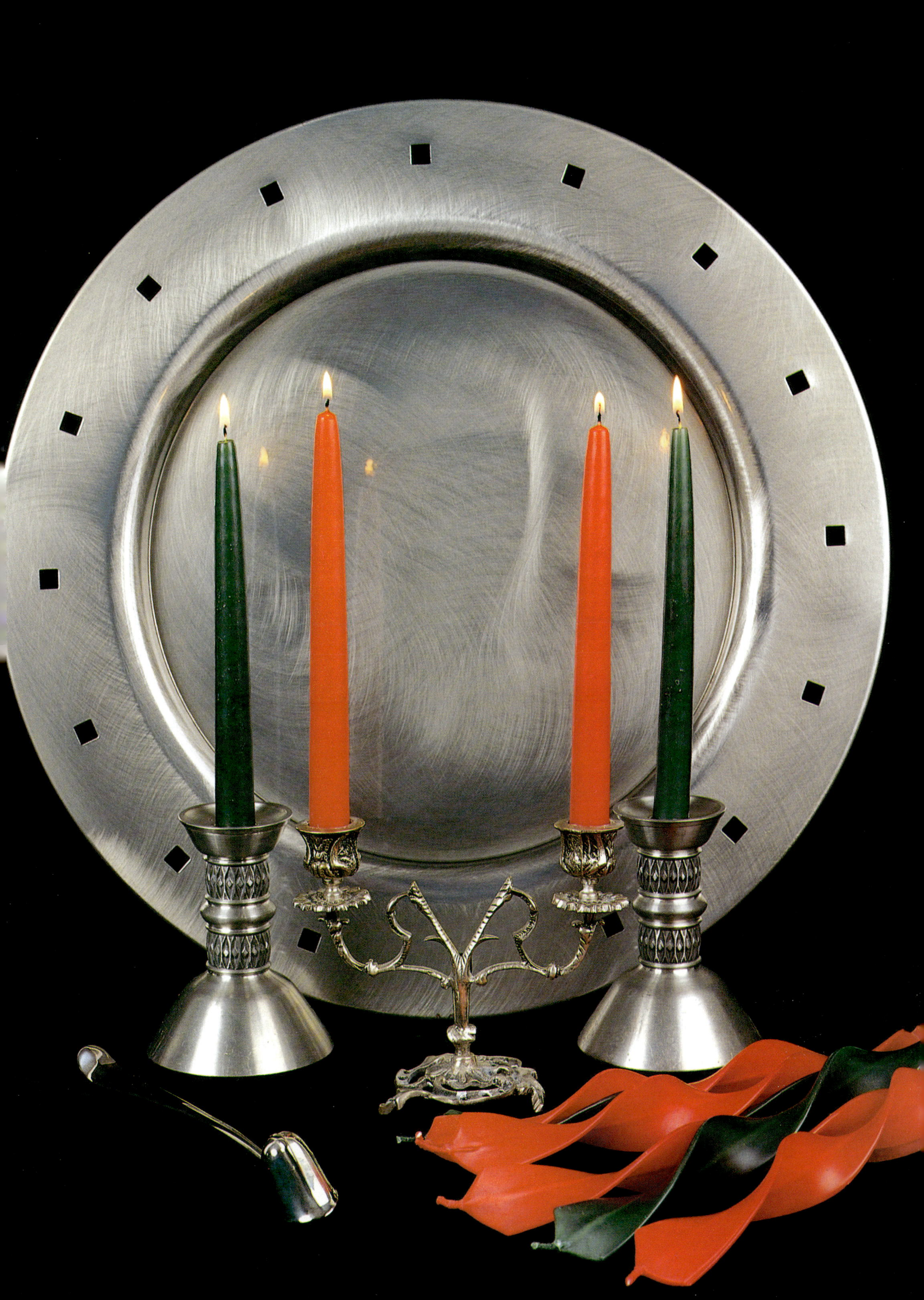

BURNS
CHAUCER
THE BLACK TULIP
ALEXANDRE DUMAS
HYMNS OF THE EARLY CHURCH
LOVE AND MR. LEWISHAM
H.G. WELLS
POETICAL WORKS OF ROBERT BROWNING
THE PROFESSOR ETC
C. BRONTË
R.L. STEVENSON
Dr. Jekyll & Mr. Hyde Fables & other Stories & Fragments
TUSITALA EDITION

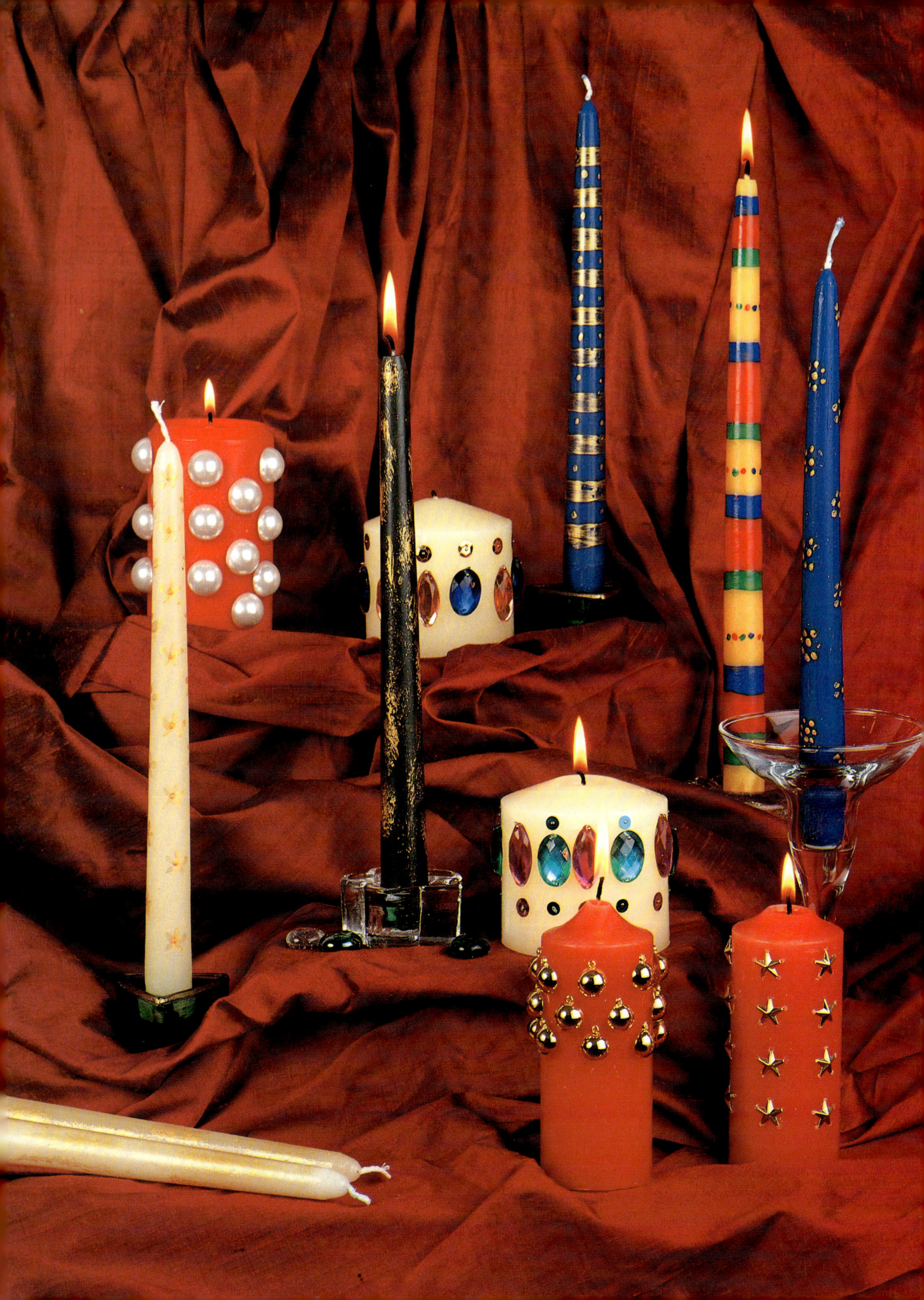

another reason for the superiority of beeswax candles – provided they were placed away from a draught, they burned with minimal attention.

Faults in the wicks were common: knots, twists or variations in wick thickness could all cause problems. One quaint handy hint, printed in 1810, tells us 'How to Remove a Thief in a Candle':

It is well known that a small knot of cotton, or as it is more commonly called, a thief, will occasion such an increased flux of the tallow, as to produce a deep guttering in a burning candle; and it is not less certain that a slip of paper, or any other substance of oblong form, about four or five inches by one, placed horizontally on the top of the candlestick, in an opposite direction, will almost instantly arrest the progress of the said thief, and prevent an subsequent effusion of the tallow.

Douters actually extinguished the flame by nipping the wick off.

Another piece of equipment related to candles in the home was the household 'save-all', a sort of small cup with a central spike, where leftover candle stubs were used up, usually in the kitchen. In the north of England, these containers were known as a 'bark', after simple trays and shallow dishes made from the bark of trees that were first used for just this purpose.

STENCILLED CANDLE

You can get a tremendous amount of satisfaction and creative pleasure by enhancing simple purchased candles with imaginative decorative treatments. Decorations add beauty to the least expensive, humblest, plain white candle and can make all the difference to a special party. And stencilling and painting add value to plain candles – once you get the hang of the techniques, you could make a bundle for the next school fete or church fund-raiser, or even sell them yourself at your local market.

The stencilled candles for this book were made with a wedding in mind, using lace and a hand-cut stencil featuring hearts. But the possible variations are as endless as your imagination and the materials you have to hand – what about 21st birthday stencils for a party, bows for a debutante reception, stars for Christmas candles, or easiest of all, initialled candles?

YOU WILL NEED

Selection of plain white or cream candles
Non-toxic gold or silver spray paint
Lengths of lace, about 5–6 cm wide, in an appropriate pattern (a scalloped edge looks nice)

Inside right: Beeswax comes in natural coloured and dyed sheets from which you can make a variety of candles (p. 52). You can use green beeswax sheets to make decorative Christmas tree candles (p. 45).

Opposite: By painting (p. 29) and stencilling (p. 33) candles you can transform any plain candle into an elegant table piece. Jewels (p. 44) and studs (p. 43) also make wonderful adornments for handmade or bought candles.

TIP
Thicker candles are the best choice for this project; narrow candles can be too fiddly to decorate this way.

TIP
You can always add more paint, but you can't take it away if you've sprayed on too much! So, be sparing.

Very thin cardboard or art paper, to make a stencil
Slim craft knife
Sticky tape

METHOD

First, plan your design. To cut a stencil, measure the height and width of the candle. Cut out a piece of thin cardboard or art paper to fit the measurements, then draw your design on it. Cut out the design using the craft knife.

Roll the stencil lightly, then fit it around the candle, joining the long edges together with sticky tape. Make sure the stencil fits very snugly. Shake the can of paint and spray evenly and lightly over the surface of stencil. Stand candle upright and set aside to dry thoroughly. When the paint is quite dry, undo the tape and gently remove the stencil.

To use lace as a stencil, simply cut lengths of lace to run around the candle in an attractive pattern, taping the edges together along the long side of candle, as for the paper stencil. Spray with gold or silver paint, leave to dry, then gently remove the tape and peel off the lace.

Note It's possible to use cut paper or cardboard stencils more than once, but the paint will clog up the lace, so if you are planning on using lace to stencil a lot of candles, make sure you buy enough lace.

ROSE CANDLE

For this project, I used a flexible rubber rose mould, purchased from a craft shop. Moulds are relatively expensive for a single use, but if correctly cared for, they can be reused many times. Rubber moulds, being softer than PVC ones, will eventually lose their shape, but they are easier for beginners to learn the technique of moulding, because you can pull and stretch them.

It is particularly important to use a cold water bath when cooling candles in flexible moulds – not only does this improve the appearance of the finished candle, but it also reduces the risk of the mould distorting if the wax cools unevenly, in a breeze, for instance.

The technique described here applies to any moulded candle, with only one important difference. If you are using a rigid mould, either a purchased one or a 'found' one, such as a milk carton, you need to add stearin, in the proportion of 10 per cent of the weight of the paraffin wax to be used. Stearin can rot rubber moulds over time, so it is not used in them.

YOU WILL NEED

A decorative flexible rose mould, made from PVC or rubber
Mould seal or Plasticine

Mould stand or frame, or a piece of stiff cardboard large enough to cover the water bath
250 g paraffin wax
1 wax dye disc
Lengths of wicking
Wicking needle
8–10 drops of the essential oil of your choice, such as rose
Double boiler
Old spoon or stirring stick
Wax thermometer
Bowl for cold water bath

The above quantities will make approximately 4 small candles.

Method

Prime the wick to fit the length of the mould, allowing about 2.5 cm extra for each open end, and set aside (see Getting Started, pages 11–12). If the mould has not come equipped with a stand or frame to hang the mould from, take a piece of stiff cardboard wide enough to cover the top of the bowl or jug you are going to use for the cooling water bath. Cut a hole in the middle of the cardboard, large enough to fit underneath the rim of the neck of the mould.

Place the paraffin wax in a double boiler or a bowl over a saucepan of simmering water and heat gently until the wax has melted. Add a few scrapings from the wax dye disc and allow to dissolve. Test for intensity of colour by dabbing a few drops of liquid coloured wax on an old plate or piece of scrap paper and wait for it to dry; add more colour, if desired. Insert the thermometer and heat the wax to 75°C (167°F).

Thread the wick through the base of the mould, using the wicking needle to punch a hole in the top end of the mould if necessary. Fix the top end of the wick snugly to the mould with mould seal, so that it is waterproof. Tug the wick gently through the open end of the mould so that it lies plumb and taut through the centre. Wind or tie the end around a wicking needle or satay stick and rest it across the top of the mould. Push the mould through the cardboard ring or purchased support and hang it over the jug or bowl.

When the wax reaches 75°C (167°F), pour it carefully into the mould, using a single, flowing movement, which will minimise air bubbles. Wait one minute, then lift the mould up by the cardboard or the support and tap it gently with a pencil or chopstick to release any air bubbles. Hang the mould over the jug or bowl and carefully pour cold water into the bowl, making quite sure no water gets into the mould and that the mould stays straight and centred.

Note Don't use the type of cool water bath described on page 18 as this method will damage the delicate petals of the rose candle.

Tip
Some manufacturers say not to bother with priming a wick for flexible moulds, but I think it makes for a smoother-burning candle.

TIP
To make the new wax adhere properly to the old, scratch the cooled hollowed surface first with a needle, then pour over the hot wax – this provides a 'grip'.

After about an hour, a slight well will have formed around the base of the candle, where the wax has shrunk as it cooled. Reheat a little of the wax and gently pour it into the hollow.

Carefully discard the water, return the mould to the stand in the jug or bowl and add more cool water. Leave the candle in place until it is quite firm – this will take at least two to three hours, depending on the size of the mould.

When the candle is cold and firm, remove the mould seal. Then remove the rubber mould by peeling it gently back on itself. If the mould is new and stubborn, rub a little dishwashing detergent or liquid soap around the outside of the mould and work it under and onto the cooled candle to help it slide off. Trim the wick straight across and even off the base of the candle, shaving or cutting off any uneven pieces of wax, cutting the wick so it rests flat on the base of the candle, and rubbing the whole candle bottom with a hot surface, such as an old iron or a hot spoon or saucepan base, so that the candle will stand perfectly straight.

PRESSED FLOWER CANDLE

Even if you don't particularly want to go the whole hog with dipping and moulding your own candles, you can unleash your creative skills by decorating the surface of purchased candles. One of the most basic techniques is to dry flowers and herbs or grasses, and use these as candle decorations.

Try to match your dried flowers or herbs to the style and look of your purchased candles. Think about the height or width of the candle, its colour – does it suggest any particular pattern to you?

To dry the flowers, either use a classic flower press or dry the flowers or herbs between sheets of absorbent paper. Another idea, which is worth trying if you are planning on drying large quantities of flowers, particularly fairly fragile ones, is to place a layer of silica gel crystals in a box, then put in the flower or herb material to be dried, then spoon in another layer of silica gel crystals, then another layer of plant material, then another layer of silica gel crystals, and so on. This is also a quicker method, with most herbs and flowers taking only a few days at the most to dry thoroughly.

YOU WILL NEED
Plain white, cream or coloured candles
A selection of dried herbs, flower heads and grasses
Quantity of paraffin wax to fill a dipping can or double boiler to the height of the tallest candle to be decorated
Iron
3 old metal-handled spoons
Cloth or clean rag

Method

Plan your design: think about what flowers or herbs you want to put where, and mark the candle with tiny pinpricks, if you wish. Lay out the plants in your chosen design on a sheet of paper, ready to apply.

Turn on the iron and stand it upright. Place three old metal-handled teaspoons against the base of the iron, with the handle side against the hot plate.

Position the flower or herb on the candle and hold it in place with one hand. Pick up one of the spoons with your other hand, using cloth or rag around your fingers so you don't get burnt. Use the hot spoon to gently 'iron' the plant material in place. Repeat, using the other heated spoons in turn as one cools, and finish applying the design. Stand the candle upright and set it aside.

Heat the wax in the dipping can or the top half of a double boiler to 95°C (205°F). Holding the candle by the wick, dip it quickly into the wax, hold for a second or two, and remove. Smooth down and into the candle any bits of plant material that are sticking out. Dip the candle again, for a second or two, then set it aside to cool completely.

Use a warm spoon to 'iron' flowers onto candle. Wear oven mitts to protect your hands when holding the heated spoon.

Are you superstitious?

Since primitive times, the idea of fire has fascinated people – not only for its practical purposes, such as cooking food and providing warmth, but also for the symbolic act of keeping darkness – where evil spirits lay in wait – at bay. It's not surprising that a wealth of superstitions and folklore has grown up around candles, lit and unlit. Candles have been associated with joy and sorrow, with birth and death and they have long been used in magical and religious rites, and as a means of divining the future. These beliefs run across all different cultures and traditions, too.

A candle flame can tell you many things:

- A blue flame means bad luck. Some say it just predicts a frost, but others say a dim blue flame is caused by a ghost passing, and it is a death omen.

- If a candle in a church blows out inexplicably, it is said to foretell the death of a clergyman. This superstition is found in many coastal areas, too, and even today, families of sailors and pilots often burn candles to ensure the safe return of their loved one, and they consider allowing a candle to gutter out a very bad omen.

- If the wick is difficult to light or won't light at all, rain is on its way. (There may be some sense in this as high humidity, which sometimes

Did you know that candles were once used to mark time at auctions? In seventeenth century England, very small, quick-burning candles, approximately 2.5 cm high, were lit when an auctioneer opened bidding on an item, and the person whose bid was last in before the candle finally guttered and went out was automatically the buyer of the item being sold. The expression **'to sell by the candle'** *is still used by some auctioneers.*

presages a thunderstorm, can cause enough dampness in the air to stop a candle from lighting properly.)

- If the wick snaps and sparks, it means strangers are coming, or it can mean a letter for the person nearest the candle at the time. A further superstition says that, if that person wanted to know when the letter would arrive, they could lick their fingertip and lightly touch the spark. If the spark stuck to the finger, the letter would arrive in a day; if the spark dropped off, the letter would take longer. Yet another superstition says that if you were to tap the candle firmly on the table, counting a day for each tap, that the spark would fall off the wick tip when the right day for the letter arriving was said aloud.

- Dreaming of a snuffed candle is a bad sign: it is a death omen. However, dreaming of a candle that is alight, or being lit, is a good omen, usually portending a birth.

- Dreaming of a brightly glowing candle means love, or news from a loved one.

- A 'winding sheet' of wax is very unlucky. This is the effect when a candle gutters as it burns, causing the wax on one side to run down unevenly. A person sitting opposite a candle with a 'winding sheet' was considered at risk of illness, or even death.

- If you blow out a candle and the wick continues to glow and smoke, bad weather is on the way. If the candle goes out completely, straight away, the weather will be fine and dry.

- If candles have been lit and left near a corpse or around a bier, beware if one inexplicably goes out. According to Irish tradition, this is a sure sign that another member of the family will die within the year.

- Leaving a candle burning in an empty room brings bad luck. The only exception to this superstition is the Christmas candle, or candles surrounding a casket. (It's probably fair to say that this superstition had its roots in plain common sense, for the bad luck could easily be a fire!)

- Never light three candles with one match. (This superstition is said to date from the First World War, when lighting three cigarettes from the one match meant that the enemy had time to take a fix on your position, take aim and fire, whereas one match strike for one cigarette did not give him enough time.)

- Never have three candles burning together in one room. Three is widely held to be an unlucky number, and three candles is a death omen (as above). However, another, contradictory superstition, tells us that three candles signifies a wedding in three months.

- Don't let a candle gutter out, as this can bring bad luck. Instead, blow or snuff it out.

- Never light a candle directly from a fire in the hearth – to do so means you will die poor. Instead, kindle a taper or light the candle from a match.

LAVENDER CANDLE

A pretty, purple candle, which gives off the sweet, fresh scent of lavender.

YOU WILL NEED

Decorative or plain rigid plastic or metal mould
Mould seal or Plasticine
Dried lavender buds, crushed lightly with a rolling pin or in a mortar and pestle (approximately 1–2 tablespoons)
250 g paraffin wax
25 g stearin
1 purple wax dye disc
Wicking
Wicking needle
8–10 drops of lavender essential oil
Double boiler
Old spoon or stirring stick
Wax thermometer
Bowl for cold water bath
Weight to hold mould in cold water bath

The above quantities will make approximately 2 candles, depending on the size of the mould used.

METHOD

Prime the wicking and set it aside (see Getting Started, pages 11–12).

Wipe out the mould with a very little vegetable oil to facilitate the removal of the moulded candle when it has cooled and hardened. Assemble the mould according to the manufacturer's instructions. Thread the wick, allowing an extra 3 cm at each end, through the base of the mould, using the wicking needle to punch a hole in the top end of the mould if necessary. Fix the top end of the wick snugly to the mould with mould seal or Plasticine, so that it is absolutely watertight. Tug the wick gently through the open end of the mould so that it lies plumb and taut through the centre. Wind or tie the end around a wicking needle or satay stick and rest it across the top of the mould. Place the mould on a piece of scrap cardboard or sheets of newspaper on a level surface.

A thousand years ago, candles were used to tell the time. A candle was divided into twelve sections, with each section known to burn for an hour, and so mark the passing of the day. These 'day candles' are still much used in churches.

Fill a double boiler with water, or improvise with a dipping can in an ordinary saucepan. Place the stearin in the double boiler and melt. Add shavings of the purple dye disc until the desired colour intensity is reached, stirring all the time with an old spoon or stirring stick. Add the paraffin wax and continue to heat. Use a wax thermometer to check when the temperature reaches 95°C (200°F). Remove the boiler from the heat (keep the two parts of the boiler together unless the temperature is too high), add a few drops of lavender essential oil and stir again.

Pour the melted wax into the mould, taking care to pour into the middle of the mould so as to get an even fill. Reserve a small amount of wax for filling the base of the candle as it cools. Leave for a minute, then gently tap the sides of the mould with a knife handle to bring any air bubbles to the top. Leave the candle to cool and harden slightly. As the candle is on the point of firming, tip in the dried lavender, about one to two tablespoonfuls, a little at a time. Use a thin wooden skewer, knitting needle or darning needle to stir the lavender evenly through the wax.

Make a cold water bath for the candle, first filling a flat-bottomed bowl or bucket with cold water to a height that will mean that, when you place the mould in it, the water will come up the sides to within 1.5 cm or so of the candle's base. Be very careful not to let any water splash inside the mould or seep in through the wicking hole. Stand the candle mould in the water bath and place a weight on top of it to keep it quite straight and stop it from bobbing around. (The weight could be an old half-brick, a full food tin, clean empty terracotta flower pots or wood chocks. Don't use books!)

As the candle cools, it will shrink slightly away from the edges of the mould and a shallow well will form in the centre. At this stage, remove the candle from the water bath, prick over the candle base with a pin or wicking needle, reheat the remaining wax to 95°C (200°F) and pour it into the centre of the candle base. Be careful not to let this new wax run down the sides of the candle where it may have pulled slightly away from the mould walls. Return the candle to the water bath and leave it to cool completely.

When the candle is quite hard, remove the mould seal, setting it aside for later use. Turn the candle out of the mould, following the manufacturer's instructions (some moulds snap apart; with others the candle should slide out). Trim the wick to about 3 cm from the top of the candle and smooth the base on a heated pie plate or slice tray.

Herb Candle

Instead of using lavender, you can create a lovely green candle using rosemary, which will also give off a wonderful scent.

You will need

Decorative or plain rigid plastic or metal mould
Mould seal or Plasticine
Dried rosemary leaves, crushed (approximately 1 tablespoon)
250 g paraffin wax
25 g stearin
Green wax dye disc
Wicking/wicking needle
8–10 drops of rosemary essential oil
Double boiler
Old spoon or stirring stick
Wax thermometer
Bowl for cold water bath
Weight to hold mould in cold water bath

The above quantities will make approximately 2 candles, depending on the size of the mould used.

Method

Prime the wicking and set it aside (see Getting Started, pages 11–12).

Wipe out the mould with a very little vegetable oil to facilitate the removal of the moulded candle when it has cooled and hardened. Assemble the mould according to the manufacturer's instructions. Thread the wick, allowing an extra 3 cm at each end, through the base of the mould, using the wicking needle to punch a hole in the top end of the mould if necessary. Fix the top end of the wick snugly to the mould with mould seal or Plasticine, so that it is absolutely water-tight. Tug the wick gently through the open end of the mould so that it lies plumb and taut through the centre. Wind or tie the end around a wicking needle or satay stick and rest it across the top of the mould. Place mould on a piece of scrap cardboard or sheets of newspaper and place on a level surface.

Fill a double boiler with water, or improvise with a dipping can in an ordinary saucepan. Place the stearin in the double boiler and melt. Add shavings of the green dye disc until the desired colour intensity is reached, stirring all the time with an old spoon or stirring stick. Add the paraffin wax and continue to heat. Use a wax thermometer to check when temperature reaches 95°C (200°F). Remove the double boiler from the heat and stir through a tablespoonful or so of crushed dried rosemary. Add 8–10 drops of rosemary essential oil and stir again.

Pour the melted wax into the mould, taking care to pour into the middle of the mould so as to get an even fill. Reserve a small amount of wax for filling the base of the candle as it cools. Leave for a minute, then gently tap the sides of the mould with a knife handle to bring any air bubbles to the top. Leave the candle to cool and harden slightly.

Make a cold water bath for the candle, filling a flat-bottomed bowl or bucket with cold water, to a height that will mean that when you place the mould in it, the water will come up the sides to within 1.5 cm or so of the candles' base. Be very careful not to let any water splash inside the mould or seep in through the wicking hole. Stand the candle mould in the water bath and place a weight on top of it to keep it quite straight and stop it from bobbing around. (The weight could be an old half-brick, a full food tin, clean empty terracotta flower pots or wood chocks. Don't use books!)

As the candle cools, it will shrink slightly away from the edges and a shallow well will form in the centre. At this stage, remove the candle from the water bath, prick over the candle base with a pin or wicking needle, reheat the remaining wax to 95°C (200°F) and pour it into the centre of the candle base. Be careful not to let this new wax run down the sides of the candle where it may have pulled slightly away from the mould walls. Return the candle to the water bath and leave it to cool completely.

When the candle is quite hard, remove the mould seal, setting it aside for later use. Turn the candle out of the mould, following the manufacturer's instructions (some moulds snap apart, with others the candle should slide out). Trim the wick to about 2 cm from the top of the candle and smooth the base on a heated pie plate or slice tray.

EGGSHELL CANDLE

This is an amusing project for adults and children alike at Easter time. Eggs are a symbol of the regeneration of life and traditionally symbolise new beginnings.

Display these dainty eggshell candles in a 'nest' made from grasses or fresh flowers, along with real eggs, or purchased egg-shaped candles for a colourful effect. Or set them in a collection of your favourite novelty egg-cups.

YOU WILL NEED

12 eggs
Lengths of wick
250 g paraffin wax
1 wax dye disc
Double boiler
Old spoon or stirring stick
Wax thermometer

METHOD

Prime the wicks and set them aside (see Getting Started, pages 11–12).
Carefully cut the tops off soft-boiled eggs, as evenly as possible.

(Eat the eggs!) Wash and dry the shells thoroughly and carefully, and remove any of the skin still adhering to the inside of the shell. If an eggshell is cracked down one side, discard it, for the wax will leak out.

Place the eggshells in egg-cups, or otherwise secure them so that they are upright. Melt the paraffin wax in the top of a double boiler, or in a bowl set in a saucepan full of simmering water. Use a wax thermometer to check when temperature reaches 57–60°C (135–140°F). Add scrapings from the colour disk until desired colour intensity is reached. Carefully and slowly pour the wax into the shells, leaving a narrow edge near the top. Leave them to cool and harden slightly.

As the candle hardens, a well will form in the centre. When the wax is still soft to the touch in the middle, and quite firm around the edges of the shell, insert a length of wick as far as you can (see floating candles, on page 32, for tips on how to insert the wick). Melt a little extra wax and use it to top up the centre of the candle. Leave the candles to cool and harden completely, and then trim the wicks to about 1 cm.

Good and Evil

Since time began nearly every human culture has considered that evil thrived in darkness, so light has been a means of keeping bad luck, illness and danger away. This is why candles and candlesticks were often found amongst items of value in coffins and burial grounds dating back to very primitive times, being included to provide comfort in the next life, as well as spiritual light to guide the person's soul. This is also the origin of the custom of keeping lighted candles around a casket before it is interred – not only do they keep evil spirits away, but they are also thought to deter the ghost of the dead person from coming back and making mischief amongst the family before it's decently buried. In Ireland it is still customary to encircle a casket with twelve candles, the idea being that evil beings cannot enter a circle of holy fire: the number twelve is significant, because it recalls the twelve Apostles.

Studded Candle

I have always enjoyed pottering around in haberdashery stores and button shops. Buttons, beads, fake jewels, artificial fruits and flowers, metal or brass decals, decorative brass studs and sequins take me back to the fun I had making bead necklaces and bracelets when I was little.

You can make wonderfully decorative candles out of something quite prosaic with the judicious application of a few studs, readily purchased from a department store or sewing shop. Depending on the size of candle you are decorating, and what you are decorating it with, use either special candle glue, melted plain wax or tiny straight pins available from haberdashery departments or sewing suppliers.

You will need

A plain thick candle: red, white or dark green all look great
Brass studs
Darning needle
A lit tea-light (night-light) candle
Thimble

Method

Set the candle to be decorated upright on a flat working surface. Warm the end of the darning needle in the tea-light flame and use it to make a small hole in the candle. Gently push the stud into the hole, using the thimble. Apply pressure evenly and, if the wax is particularly hard, ease the stud out again and repeat the step with the darning needle, this time making the hole a little deeper. If the purchased candle is old or very hard-milled, it may flake or crack if you just try to push the stud in without preparing the wax. Press in the studs in a decorative pattern – perhaps in simple rings around the candle, or in vertical or horizontal lines.

Variation Why not make your own studs and jewels to appliqué on the sides of a purchased or moulded candle? Some of the larger craft shops sell a wide variety of rigid plastic moulds of tiny decorative shapes – suns, stars, flowers, for instance – that are filled, allowed to cool and then glued to the sides of a candle by coating both the candle surface and the back of the piece to be applied with wax glue or a little melted plain wax. You can improvise with tiny metal jelly moulds or agar-agar sweet moulds, such as those found in Asian grocery stores. Work quickly and press the wax stud into place with a minimum of wax, holding it firmly until secure, and so avoiding a built-up hump beneath the stud.

Jewelled Candle

There's a tremendous amount of satisfaction to be gained from decorating plain moulded or rolled candles with imaginative decorations. Here, I've used glass-headed dressmaker's pins, sequins and purchased fake jewels. Don't let your ideas stop there, though – consider the possibilities of tiny silver bells and lengths of pearl beading for a wedding table display, or artificial red rose-buds for a Valentine's dinner.

You will need

Purchased candle in shape and colour of choice
Glass-headed dressmaker's pins
Sequins
Fine-headed dressmaker's pins
Costume jewels or glass beads cut cabochon-style, that is, with flat backs

Tip

Don't use regular-sized pins. Not only are they too long, and end up poking through the other side of your candle, but they usually 'dig' a hole as they are pressed in. Use finer, shorter pins to secure studs and fake jewels if they do not already have a spike.

Additional plain candle in matching colour
Lit tea-light (night-light) candle
A small amount of wax to melt
Small fine-tipped paint brush

Method

Set the candle to be decorated on a flat work surface. You might want to make pinprick markings on the candle where you want to apply the jewels and sequins, to ensure they are equally spaced if you have a very precise design in mind, such as horizontal lines.

To apply sequins, simply press them in place and push a fine-headed dressmaking pin through the centre hole of each sequin. If necessary, warm the pin slightly in the lit tea-light candle flame to facilitate pushing it into the candle wax. To apply flat-backed glass beads or jewels, melt broken chunks of additional plain candle in a matching colour in a double boiler over simmering water. Dip a paintbrush in melted wax and use it to paint the back of the jewel or bead and so hold it in place.

Christmas Tree Candle

Beeswax sheets are available in several different colours, including red and green. Here's an easy idea for Christmas time – display these little Christmas tree candles as a group, range them along a mantelpiece, or use them as placemarkers at the dinner table.

You will need

2–3 sheets dark green textured beeswax
Sharp, narrow-bladed knife, such as craft knife
Glitter
Tiny glass-headed pins or sequins
Primed wick
8–10 drops of pine essential oil

The above quantities make 8–12 candles.

Method

Use purchased primed wicking or prepare primed wicking yourself (see Getting Started, pages 11–12).

To make four candles, you will need four rectangles of dark green beeswax, measuring about 5 x 40 cm. Cut the first sheet to obtain the four rectangles. Lightly score, and then cut, each rectangle diagonally, from corner to corner, using the sharp-bladed knife. You will now have eight long thin triangles. Sprinkle each with a few drops of pine oil. Thickly spread the glitter on a tray or plate, and press the long diagonal edge into the glitter. Cut a piece of primed wick about 6 cm long, place it against the short edge of the triangle and firmly roll the triangle

---

A very old candle superstition is linked to modern-day Halloween trick-or-treating. This was the English custom of 'Lating the Witches', which was practised up until the early nineteenth century. The idea was to give each member of the village a lighted candle on Halloween and let them walk the streets between 11 o'clock and midnight. If a person's candle stayed alight, it boded well, but if it blew out continually, it was a bad omen.

from this edge to the point, making a conical tree shape. Decorate the tree with glass-headed pins or sequins.

Give an even finish to the base of your candles by heating a metal pie dish or slice tray over a low flame, then pressing the base of the candle against the hot metal, taking care to hold the candle upright. This seals the layers of beeswax together and gives a smooth finish.

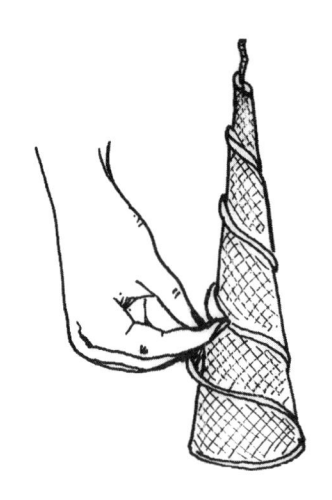

Use your thumb and forefinger to spread edge of a rolled tapered candle.

CHRISTMAS CANDLES

At Christmas time, it is lucky to place a special, fat Christmas candle in the centre of the room and keep it burning all through the night of Christmas Eve. It should be lit by the head of the household, or the oldest member of the family, and blown or snuffed out by that person first thing in the morning. This is thought to ensure prosperity for the coming year.

Another old superstition, dating from at least early medieval times, is related to the idea of the Christmas candle. This calls for a large candle to be lit and placed in a window where it is visible to all passers-by, and left to burn all night to be blown out on Christmas morning. This tradition recalls the story of the Holy Family, seeking shelter at Christmas time. It was also once believed that no stranger who was attracted to the light should ever be turned away on this special night, in case it was Jesus Christ himself, returning to test humanity.

MOSAIC CANDLE

These jewel-coloured candles look as though they would be complicated to make but they are, in fact, one of the easiest candles to create. A Mosaic Candle is a great project for beginners to start with for two reasons: first, you can't really make any mistakes, and second, you can use up all sorts of left-over bits of both bought and made candles you may have handy. In fact, after you've been making candles for even a short while, you'll find that you're really grateful for a project that will use up all those bits and pieces of unused wax in different amounts and colours! You can work with just two colours, but a prettier effect is usually obtained with a larger number of colours.

YOU WILL NEED

1 rigid mould, cylindrical, star or pyramid shape, or straight-sided square or rectangle
Mould seal or Plasticine
Appropriate length of wick, about 20 cm
Wicking needle
Selection of chunks of different-coloured wax
225 g paraffin wax

25 g stearin
1 wax dye disc, a light colour such as white or yellow, for preference, or select wax in a contrasting colour (see note on colour selection)
Essential oil of your choice, such as patchouli, lemon and ylang-ylang (approximately 8–10 drops)
Double boiler
Old spoon or stirring stick
Wax thermometer
Bowl for a cool water bath
Weight to hold mould in cold water bath

Method

Prime the wick (see Getting Started, pages 11–12).

Prepare the mould by threading the wick through the hole in the base of the mould with the wicking needle and then tying it at the open end, around the wicking needle. Pull the wick so it falls straight and firm through the centre of the mould. Use a piece of mould seal or Plasticine to secure the wick at the other end, making quite sure it is absolutely watertight.

Break up the coloured wax lumps into different-sized chunks, using a rolling pin. The best effects are realised when you use different sizes and shapes of wax. Put the chunks into a mould, carefully arranging them so that there are not too many large air spaces. Set aside.

Put the stearin into a double boiler or a bowl over a saucepan of hot water and heat gently until it melts. Add shavings from the wax dye disc and stir with a stirring stick or old spoon until the shavings have dissolved. Add the paraffin wax and continue to stir. Add a few more shavings from the disc if you want to intensify the colour. Add 8–10 drops of essential oil, or oil blend, of your choice. Place a wax thermometer in the mixture and heat the wax to 80°C (180°F).

When the wax is at the right temperature, pour it into the mould over the chunks of wax. Pour slowly and evenly to ensure all the spaces are filled with wax and to minimise any air getting trapped in the mould. It's possible, with practice, to release air pockets as you go, by stopping pouring and gently manoeuvring the problem piece of wax with a skewer, knitting needle or piece of fuse wire.

Set the mould aside for a minute or two, then tap gently and firmly all around the mould with a knife handle – this will help to remove any unseen air bubbles. Make a cool water bath for the candle, first filling a flat-bottomed bowl or bucket with cold water to a height that will mean that, when you place the mould in it, the water will come up the sides to within 1.5 cm or so of the candle base. Be very careful not to let any water splash inside the mould or seep in through the wicking hole. Stand the candle mould in the water bath and place a weight on top of it to keep it quite straight and stop it from bobbing around. (The weight could be an old half-brick, a full food tin, clean empty terracotta flower pots or wood chocks. Don't use books!)

Colour selection

Many different options are available when you are making a mosaic candle, depending, of course, on what colour bits and pieces of wax you have to start with. If you have several different colours and shapes, try plain white or yellow wax. If the majority of the pieces are blue and green, choose pale blue as your filling wax; if they are orange and brown, fill with yellow; pink and red chunks look pretty when filled with green.

Tip

Wax temperature is critical with all candlemaking projects, but is particularly so with mosaic candles. Do not let the wax temperature exceed 80°C (180°F), as too-hot wax will cause partial melting of some, but not all of the chunks, making for a muddy appearance.

*C*andlemas Day falls on 2 February. It is also known as the Day of the Presentation of Our Lord in the Catholic Church. Traditionally, on this day, all the candles that are to be used during the coming year are consecrated. The light of a candle in church is said to symbolise Jesus Christ, called 'the light of the world' and 'a light to lighten the Gentiles' in the Bible. Western and Eastern churches commemorate Candlemas Day with candlelit processions. Many old weather proverbs relate to Candlemas Day, including these two:

'If Candlemas Day be dry and fair,
Then half o' winter's come and more,
If Candlemas Day be wet and foul,
The half o'winter was gone at Yule.'
Scottish proverb

'The badger peeps out of his hole on
Candlemas Day,
and if he finds snow, he walks abroad –
but if he sees the sun shining, he draws
back into his hole.'
German proverb

Opposite: *Floating candles (p. 31) make a wonderful table centrepiece when they are placed in a large glass bowl filled with water and flower petals.*

As the candle cools it will shrink – after about an hour, a shallow well will have formed around the base of the wick. To avoid having a hollow up the middle and to get a more professional finish to your candle, remove the candle from the water bath and pierce the indentation several times with the wicking needle. Then heat a little extra wax and pour it into the well. Be careful not to use too much extra wax or it will run down the outside of the candle and ruin its appearance.

Return the candle to the cold water bath, secure with a weight again, and leave for another hour or two until it is quite set. Peel off the candle mould seal, and the candle should slip easily out of the mould. Trim the wick flat across the base of the candle. For a professional finish, heat an old metal spoon and use it to rub over the base of the candle where the wick is, to make it smooth. Trim the top of the wick. Polish your candle by rubbing over it with an old soft cloth that has been dipped in a small amount of vegetable oil.

Medieval Candle

For this project, I used a flexible rubber mould with a decorative raised surface, purchased from a craft shop. These moulds are relatively expensive for a one-off use, but if correctly cared for, they can be reused many times. Rubber moulds, being softer than PVC ones, will eventually soften and lose their shape, but they are easier for beginners to learn the technique of moulding, because you can pull and stretch them.

It is particularly important to use a cold water bath when cooling candles in flexible moulds – not only does this improve the appearance of the finished candle, but it also reduces the risk of the mould distorting if the wax cools unevenly, in a breeze, for instance.

The technique described can apply to any moulded candle, with only one important difference. If you are using a rigid mould – either a purchased one or a found one, such as a milk carton – you need to add stearin, in the proportion of about 10 per cent of the weight of the paraffin wax to be used. Stearin can rot rubber moulds over time, so it is not used in them.

You will need

A decorative flexible mould, made from PVC or rubber
Mould seal or Plasticine
Mould stand or frame, or a piece of stiff cardboard large enough to cover the water bath
250 g Paraffin wax
25 g stearin
1 wax dye disc, such as purple or magenta
Wick
Wicking needle

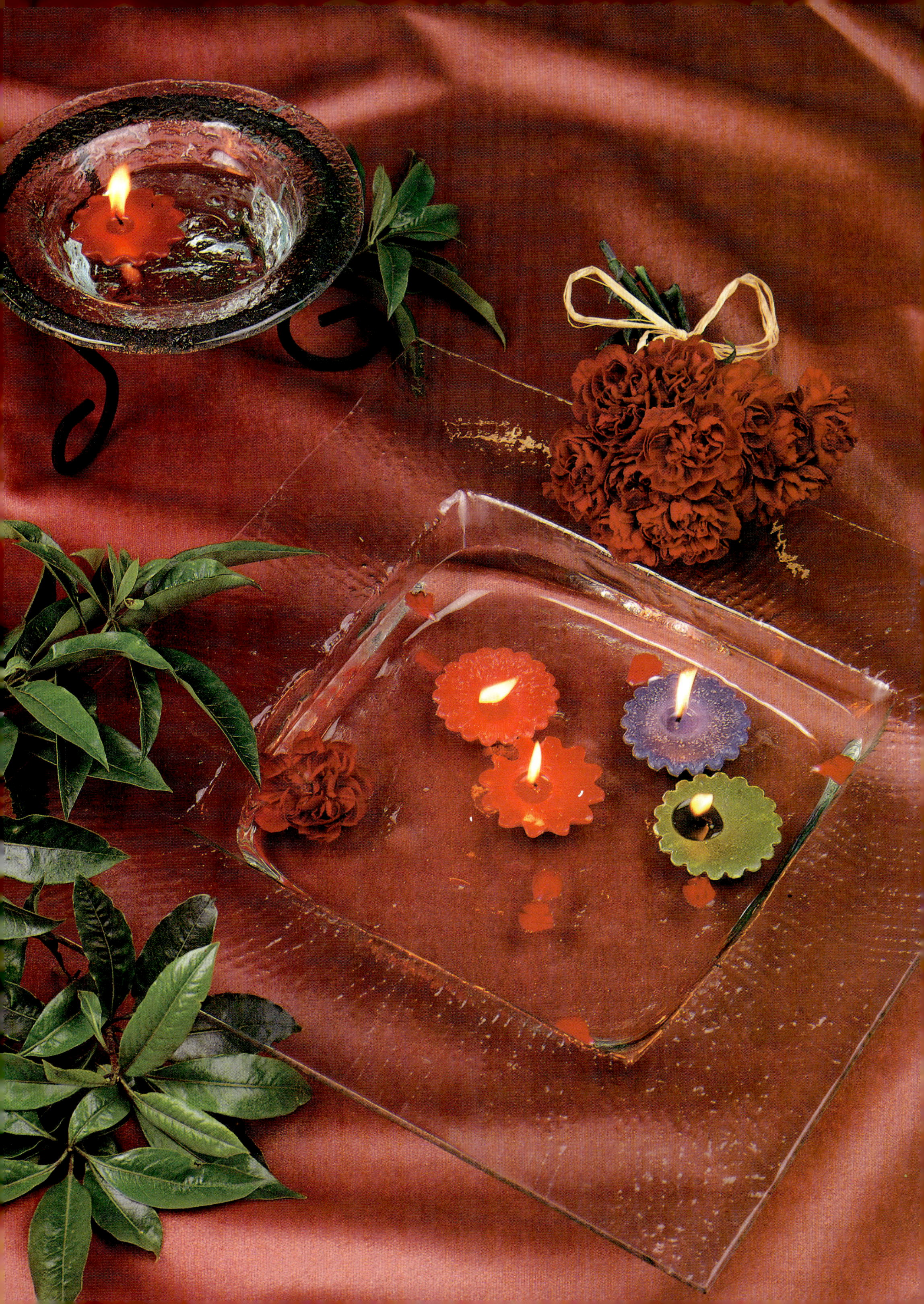

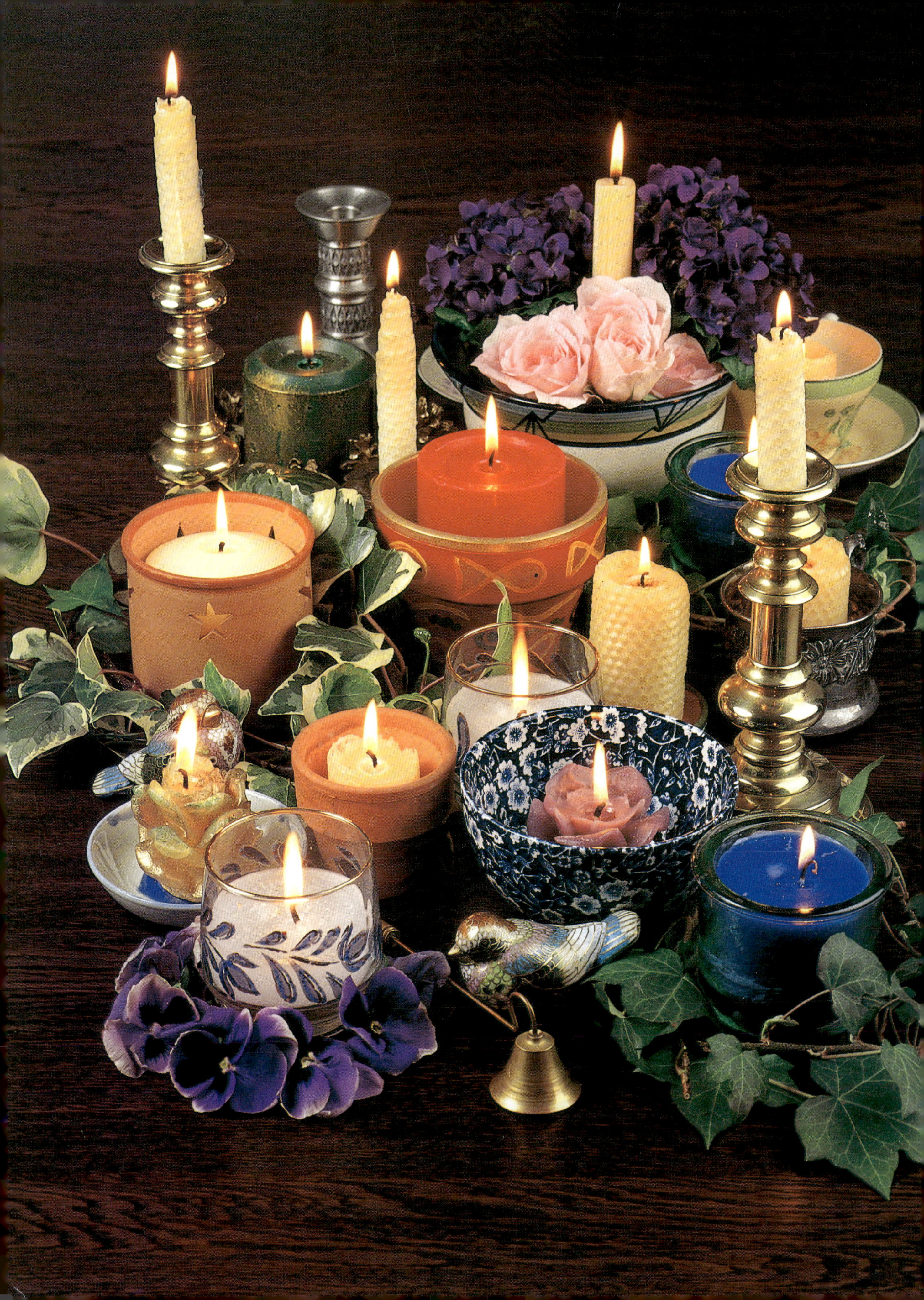

8–10 drops of an essential oil of your choice, such as rose or patchouli
Fine paintbrush or sponge applicator
Non-toxic antique gold paint
Double boiler
Old spoon or stirring stick
Wax thermometer
Bowl for cold water bath

The above quantities will make approximately 3–4 candles.

Method

Prime the wick to fit the length of the mould (see Getting Started, pages 11–12), allowing about 3 cm extra for each open end, and set aside. Some manufacturers say not to bother with priming a wick for flexible moulds, but I think it makes for smoother burning.

If the mould has not come equipped with a stand or frame to hang the mould from, take a piece of stiff cardboard wide enough to cover the top of the bowl you are going to use for the cooling water bath. Cut a hole in the middle of the cardboard, large enough to fit underneath the rim of the neck of the mould.

Put the paraffin wax in a double boiler or a bowl over a saucepan of simmering water and heat gently until the wax has melted. Add a few scrapings from the wax dye disc and allow to dissolve. Test the intensity of the colour by dabbing a few drops of liquid coloured wax on an old plate or piece of scrap paper and wait for it to dry; add more colour, if desired. Insert the thermometer and heat the wax to 75°C (167°F).

Thread the primed wick through the base of the mould, using the wicking needle to punch a hole in the top end of the mould if necessary. Fix the top end of the wick snugly to the mould with mould seal or Plasticine, so that it is absolutely watertight. Tug the wick gently through the open end of the mould so that it lies plumb and taut through the centre. Wind or tie the end of the wicking around a wicking needle or satay stick and rest it across the top of the mould. Push the mould through the cardboard ring or purchased support, and hang it over the bowl.

When the wax reaches 75°C (167°F), pour it carefully into the mould, using a single, flowing movement to minimise air bubbles. Wait one minute, then lift the mould up by its cardboard or support and tap gently with a pencil or chopstick to release any air bubbles. Hang the mould over the bowl and carefully pour in cold water, making quite sure no water gets into the mould and that the mould stays straight and centred.

After about an hour, a slight well will have formed around the base of the candle, where the wax has shrunk as it cools. Reheat a little of the wax and gently pour into the hollow. To ensure that the new wax sticks properly to the old, scratch the cooled hollowed surface of the

Opposite: *Almost anything can be used as a candle holder: decorated glasses, terracotta pots, bowls, tea cups and saucers, or the more traditional brass and pewter candlesticks.*

candle first with a needle, then pour over the hot wax – this provides a grip.

Carefully discard the water, return the mould to the stand in the bowl and add more cool water. Leave the candle until it is quite firm – this will take at least two to three hours, depending on the size of the mould.

When the candle is cold and firm, remove the mould seal. Then remove the rubber mould by peeling it gently back on itself. If the mould is new and stubborn, rub a little dishwashing detergent or liquid soap around the outside of the mould and work it under and onto the candle to help it slide off. Trim the wick straight across and even off base of candle, shaving or cutting off uneven pieces of wax, cutting the wick so it rests flat on the base of the candle, and rubbing the candle bottom with a hot surface, such as an old iron or a hot spoon or saucepan base, so that the candle will stand perfectly straight.

Decorate the completed candle with gold paint, using a paintbrush or sponge roller to apply it. Polish with a dampened cloth, or a rag dipped in a little vegetable oil. Don't try to create a perfect design – the appeal of painted details is that they should look hand-done, not as though they've been evenly stamped on by a machine.

Now you're ready to experiment with painting other moulded candles – beehives, roses, whatever takes your fancy! Again, the appeal of these candles lies not only in their shape but in the attention you give to picking out the details of their moulding.

TIP
When painting a finish on a candle, use poster paint or other water-based paint or professional candle paint. Check with the supplier that the paint you buy to decorate your moulded candle does not give off toxic fumes when burnt – most manufacturers specify on the back of the tube or packet whether this is so. Refer also to painted candles, on pages 29–31.

CANDLES IN CHURCH

Apart from being used for domestic lighting, candles have also been much used for religious purposes. Candles were used in church services in many ways: the lighting of them for reading the Gospel, the placing of a lighted taper in a child's hand at baptism, as well as great religious rituals like Easter, where the church decreed that candles be lit and burnt continuously for days at a time. At Canterbury Cathedral in 1457, an enormous Paschal candle 'so lofty it had to be kindled by a light let down from the vault of the choir' was used to commemorate the Feast of the Ascension.

In particular, candles made from beeswax have a long history of use in churches and cathedrals. This was partly because they were less smoky than tallow ones, and they also had a brighter flame and a pleasant odour. There was also a symbolic significance, for the bee was considered to be blessed by God, providing man with two wonderful gifts – honey and wax – and also providing a shining example of industry! Beeswax continues to be used widely because of its superior burning qualities.

> The Catholic Church has ruled that candles on the High Altar of any Catholic church have to contain at least 65 per cent beeswax, with the remainder being allowed to be made of tallow. Other, less important, altars could use candles with no more than 25 per cent beeswax.

Shell Candles

Nearly every household has a collection of shells that can be used to make these practical and pretty candles. The easiest method of all is probably just to wash and recycle a dozen empty oyster shells, or if you want to make a lot of little candles for a party, for instance, you could ask your local fishmonger for discarded shells from mussels, oysters, or even scallops.

Pick over the shells and use common sense to decide which are going to be the most useful for your purpose – shells that are almost completely flat will not hold enough wax, while cracked or broken ones are obviously not suitable. Look for shells with deepish cavities that will hold plenty of wax and a wick. If you want to go all the way with the seaside theme, you could display them together with extra shells, sand and even pieces of driftwood.

You will need

A selection of shells (see above for hints)
Mould seal or Plasticine
Lengths of wick
Wooden toothpicks or thick pins
250 g paraffin wax
25 g stearin (for coloured candles only)
1 wax dye disc (for coloured candles only)
Double boiler
Old spoon or stirring stick
Wax thermometer

This quantity of wax will make approximately 8 candles.

Method

Wash and scrub out the shells as thoroughly as possible. Set aside until they are completely dry – if you have convoluted shells, hold a hairdrier at the opening of the shell to make quite sure no droplets of water are left inside. When they are dry, place the shells on a flat surface (an old pastry block or chopping board is ideal) and secure with mould seal or Plasticine to keep them quite level.

Cut the wicks into short lengths and secure in a blob of mould seal in the middle of base of the shells. Depending on the shell, you can

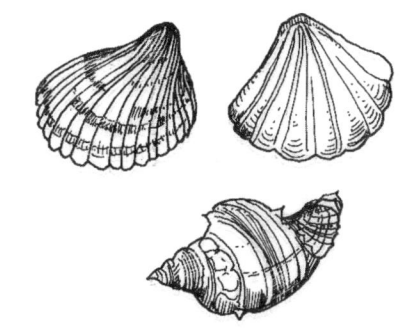

TIP
A spouted ladle can be handy here, as it takes practice to tip the saucepan up evenly and you can ruin a shell if the wax slops over.

In the past beeswax candles were made according to specialist techniques, and required far more work than making tallow ones. For candlemaking, beeswax was usually first whitened by bleaching. To accomplish this, the wax was melted in hot water, pressed through finely woven cloth and then moulded into flat cakes. These were laid out in the open air and turned occasionally, so that sun and air were able to turn the wax a semi-transparent whitish colour, and soften the smell. Then, rather than being dipped into a cauldron, a workman 'dressed' the candles by hand, using a long-handled ladle to pour hot beeswax down the sides of individual wicks, one by one, until the required thickness was achieved. Each candle was then smoothed into shape, by hand, while still soft, with special hardwood rollers, usually made from box wood.

---

just lean the wick up and over the edge of a shell, but if it is a flattish shell you will need to keep it upright so that it will not fall into the liquid wax when it is poured in. To do this (and again, depending on the size of the shell), thread the wick onto a thick pin or twist it around a wooden toothpick before pressing this into the mould seal, to act as a support.

White candles To make plain white shell candles, place the paraffin wax in the double boiler and melt; use the thermometer to check when the temperature reaches 80°C (180°F). Carefully pour the melted wax into the shells and around the wicks or supports. Don't fill the shell right to the brim: leave a little space around the edge of the top of the shells.

Leave the shell candles to harden and cool – check in about 45 minutes. As the wax cools it will shrink away a little from the sides and a hollow will form at the top. Prick the tops of the candles gently with a needle or pin, melt a little extra paraffin wax to 80°C (180°F) and use it to top up the candles and fill the space around the edge.

Coloured candles To make coloured shell candles, place stearin in the top of the double boiler and add shavings from the dye disc until you have the desired intensity of colour, stirring with old spoon or stirring stick. Add the paraffin wax and heat to 80°C (180°F). Then proceed according to the instructions above for making white shell candles.

BEESWAX CANDLES

These are very simple candles to make – all you have to do is roll a sheet of prepared wax around a wick. Every first-time candle maker and even the youngest child can roll a respectable beeswax candle!

Beeswax sheets are readily available in craft shops in preformed honeycomb sheets, usually measuring about 25 x 40 cm. The colour will vary, depending on the supplier and the area the wax comes from, from cream to almost white, through all shades of yellow to a quite dark golden brown. You can also buy beeswax sheets that have been dyed bright colours, such as blue, green and red.

The other equipment you will need you probably have already – a hairdrier, a sharp thin knife, a ruler (preferably metal) and scissors, plus some round wicking. Make sure you have a firm, smooth surface for rolling the sheets up on. A piece of old Laminex or smooth plywood is perfect – rolling on a tablecloth or old blanket is not a good idea because the wax will pick up lint and fluff. Apart from being a fire hazard in the finished candle, these bits of fluff will dull the finished appearance of the candle. Another important point to remember in making beeswax candles is to roll the candles as firmly and tightly as possible. Air trapped between the sheets will make the candle smoke more than it does with regular moulded candles. Remember to always set the candles on a candlestick or protective base, because they will drip more than moulded candles, and they burn faster, too.

The candles I made for this book are plain – I quite like the honeycombed surface and think that is decoration enough. However, it's easy and fun to experiment with decorating beeswax candles by cutting strips of the contrasting natural or coloured shades and wrapping or winding them around the outside of the finished candle – tying a 'bow' made from a 'ribbon' of beeswax is another idea. Or you could cut out a series of different-sized hearts from a sheet of red beeswax, gently warm the pieces and press them in a spiral around the sides of a tall slim cream beeswax candle.

This is a terrific project for even very young children. Adult supervision is, however, required with the use of the scalpel or craft knife.

YOU WILL NEED

Sheets of beeswax
Hairdrier
Sharp craft knife or scalpel
Scissors
A heavy rule
Lengths of wick
Essential oil or oil blend, such as lemon or lemon-scented tea-tree

METHOD

Prime the lengths of wick and set them aside (see Getting Started, pages 11–12).

Straight-sided candles To make a straight-sided candle, measure and cut a rectangle about 10 x 20 cm. (The short side of the sheet will be the height of the candle, so you can vary the size of your candles by starting with larger sheets, if you prefer.) Cut the wick to the height of the candle plus about 2 cm to extend beyond the top of the finished rolled candle.

Set the hairdrier on a low setting and play it over the wax sheet to soften it slightly. Lay the wick along one of the short edges and press it gently, using the warmth of your fingertips to just hold in place. Sprinkle a few drops of essential oil or oil blend of your choice over the wax sheet. Make your first turn to roll up your candle, being sure to press evenly and firmly around the wick – a snug first turn will give a successful result. Then continue to roll towards the end of the sheet, applying even pressure and finishing on a straight line.

To finish, press the edge of the wax sheet into the side of the candle. Trim the base of the candle so that it is flat and neatly squared-off.

Tapered candles To make a tapered beeswax candle, measure and cut a rectangle about 10 x 20 cm. Cut the rectangle in two across the diagonal.

Warm the first sheet with the hairdrier, as described for the

TIP

When making beeswax candles, work in a warm room, with a temperature of about 25°C (80°F). This makes the beeswax easier to handle and also helps the sheet adhere to itself as you roll. If the sheet sides are not snugly flattened against each other, the finished candle will not burn evenly.

straight-sided beeswax candles, and lay a length of wick along the short side of the diagonal, making sure that the wick extends about 2 cm past the end of the wax sheet. Press the wick into place and sprinkle with essential oil or oil blend of your choice. Roll the edge of the sheet over the wick, checking that you have a snug fit and that the wick is held closely with no air bubbles, then continue to roll smoothly and evenly towards pointed end.

When you reach the end, press the loose edge of the wax into the side of the candle, trim the wick, and trim and flatten the base, as described for the straight-sided beeswax candles.

Repeat the process with the second diagonal sheet, this time laying it the other way around so that the two candles are the mirror-image of each other and form a pair.

To finish, you can leave the tapered beeswax candles as they are, or make a graceful fluted edge by running your thumb and forefinger gently along the cut diagonal edge of the candle, flaring it out as it spirals down the side of the candle. Once you get the hang of this, try dipping your fingertips in glitter as you go, pressing the glitter into the wax as you warm it with your hands. Beeswax has a slightly tacky finish so the glitter should stick quite well without the use of glue.

Variations A deceptively simple and clever idea is to make up the tapered beeswax candles using two sheets of beeswax in contrasting colours. Cut one diagonal in one colour and another, slightly longer, in another colour. Align the bases, then roll up evenly.

You can also experiment with making larger spiral candles in a number of colours, using up to six or seven sheets of beeswax at once. One very attractive idea is to capitalise on the variations of colour found in natural beeswax itself. For instance, take three sheets of natural honey-coloured beeswax, then one each of a pale cream, medium tan and the darkest natural brown you can find. Other effective colour combinations are red, white and green for a Christmas candle, or red and white.

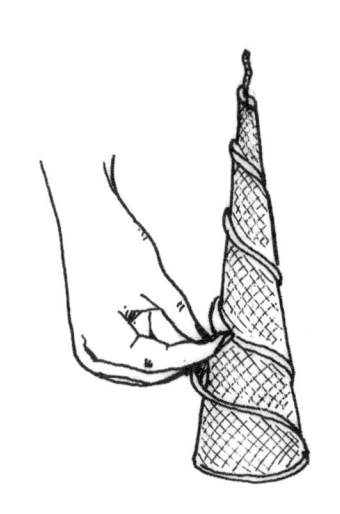

Use your thumb and forefinger to spread edge of a rolled tapered candle

Starry Candles

With most creative pursuits, whether you're cooking, or painting, sewing a dress or decorating a room, it's almost invariably the simple ideas that work the best – the one delicious sauce instead of a range of condiments, the simple line of a well-cut skirt or coat, the one vase of beautiful fresh flowers instead of a bench full of ornaments. So it is with this idea!

You will need
2 slim black or cream candles
Gold paint
Fine-tipped paintbrush

Method

Wipe over the candles with a clean soft cloth to remove any dust or grease.

Using gold paint and a fine-tipped paintbrush, paint small gold stars all over the candle. These can either be asterisk-style (easiest for the beginner – just mark a dot and draw lines out from it!) or, if you feel confident, draw the stars freehand and fill them in. Display in brass candlesticks or holders for extra impact.

Happy Birthday!

Probably the best-known candle traditions of all concern the birthday cake. The custom of decorating birthday cakes with candles goes back to the days of ancient Greece, when worshippers of Artemis, goddess of the hunt who was also associated with both chastity and childbirth, offered honey cakes to her at temple altars on the sixth day of every month, which was said to be her special day. These cakes were round, like the moon which was Artemis' symbol, and dotted with lit tapers, which were said to be emblematic of stars.

The custom of blowing out birthday candles, as we know it today, dates from the Middle Ages, when German families would light a candle for the birthday child when he or she awoke, and the child would blow it out at the end of the day. From this came the idea of using the same number of candles as the birthday child had years – one variation saw an extra candle being placed on the cake, as a superstition to keep the 'light of life' burning. And, just as is the case today, if the child could blow out all the candles in one go, it meant good luck and a wish come true for the next year.

*Wishes, luck and candles have always been related. Blowing out the candles is assumed to bring good luck – and a wish come true – to the birthday celebrant for the coming year (provided they blow out **all** the candles with one breath and do not tell anyone what they wished for). This custom originated with the ancient Greeks, for whom a candle symbolised a life.*

Treasure Candles

Whenever I make candles, the little girl that I used to be, who loved to play with clay and Plasticine and make all sorts of shapes, is never far away. I still like to play with wax, and I enjoy its many moods and secrets. Here are some ideas for making candles with hidden treasures that children will love to make and share with their friends.

Method

Moulded treasure candles Take a plain square or pyramid-shaped rigid candle mould and wick up and lightly oil, as usual (see page 39 for details on using rigid moulds). When you've melted and coloured the wax, drop in four or five small heat-proof charms, such as cabochon beads, or a small brass-plated star or wizard, or a nicely shaped pebble.

*One of the loveliest candle customs comes from America. Each Christmas Eve, hundreds of **luminarias** are lit around the town of Albuquerque, New Mexico, along paths, along roof tops and even down streets and driveways. These **luminarias** are simply formed by half-filling paper bags with sand and securing a candle in the centre, then folding down the top of the bag in a sort of 'cuff' to stop the wind from blowing out the flame. The flickering light through the brown paper makes a pretty, delicate glowing spectacle. No one is quite sure where the custom originated, though some say it came from Spain. The idea is that the **luminarias** show the spirit of the Christ Child the way to the town.*

Gift and craft shops have an enormous selection of such novelties. Mould the candle as usual and allow to cool. Write a little card or scroll to accompany the candle, perhaps writing a little story or poem about the lucky charms that will come to light as the candle burns down.

Beeswax candles When rolling straight-sided beeswax candles (see page 53), warm the sheet of wax as usual, then place it flat on a piece of plain paper (not newspaper) which you have scattered thickly with glitter. Press down firmly so that the glitter adheres to that side. Roll up the candle around the wick, with the glitter side outermost. If the glitter candle is to be a gift, tie it up with glitter-string or shiny silver ribbon.

Moulded candles with foil Here's a pretty use for left-over pieces of coloured foil (such as the inner layers of lolly wrappings). Collect pieces of foil, no matter how small, or even if they're torn. Crumple lightly, so that they have a crinkled, not crushed, look. Prepare a rigid mould, wiping it out very lightly with vegetable oil, wicking up with a primed wick, and securing with mould seal (see page 39 for instructions on making candles in moulds). Pour in a small amount of melted wax (uncoloured, or with just a touch of very pale blue or pink so you can see the foils) and swirl it around the sides of the mould. While the wax is still warm and starting to become firm, press pieces of foil lightly over the walls of the mould. Fill the mould with the rest of the wax and refill base of the mould as candle cools. You can also just mix the scraps of foil into melted wax mixture and pour straight into mould, but by arranging them first, you tend to see more of the pretty colours and avoid having them all clump up around the wick neck of the mould.

FROM CANDLESTICKS TO CHANDELIERS

In the past ornate candle holders, such as hanging candelabra and wall brackets or sconces, were generally found only in wealthy homes. Over the centuries, candlesticks have been confused with candelabra, wall-lights and chandeliers; in addition, a distinction has not always been clearly drawn between a holder for an oil-lamp and one for a candle.

An example is the biblical seven-branched candelabrum, or menorah, provided by Moses for the Ark of the Covenant. It was described in the Book of Exodus (37:17) as 'a candlestick of pure gold' ornamented with flowers and rounded studs or bosses. It was further described as having 'six branches going out of the sides thereof; three branches of the candlestick out of the one side thereof, and three branches of the candlestick out of the other side thereof'. What all this means is that it had, in fact, one central support and two sets of three side branches, each of the seven holding a small vessel containing oil and a wick.

The first candlesticks were very simple, functional objects – maybe no more than a suitably shaped piece of wood or stone, or moulded clay. Apart from those used by the Romans, the earliest decorative candlesticks we know of date from the eleventh and twelfth centuries AD, and, like the majority of candlesticks made during the following centuries, they were largely for ecclesiastical use.

Large hanging fittings of candlesticks were particularly in evidence as the more ritualistic ceremonies of the Christian era began to demand a more flamboyant style of decorating and furnishing. A pair of silver candlesticks is recorded as having been presented to Henry III in Westminster Abbey in 1250, while, in the 1400s, Henry VI had a pair made of gold, set with four sapphires, four rubies, four emeralds and twenty-four pearls. Of course, wars and other upheavals have periodically resulted in the destruction of valuables, often those belonging to the church, so many of these earlier gorgeous candlesticks have been lost.

All these candlesticks and candle holders were once called chandeliers – which came to refer to anything that held a candle, not just the complex light fittings we know today. A chandelier d'appliqué was a bracket for hanging on a wall and was introduced during the fourteenth century. A chandelier à fleurs was a candlestick with floral patterns in coloured enamel or gilt, while a chandelier à personnage fleurs, in bronze, silver or wood, was a life-size or half-life-size figure of a servant holding a candlestick. Early Renaissance candlesticks stood on three scrolled feet, and were made of either bronze, brass or wood. Such large candlesticks were found in home and church alike. By Tudor times in England, the well-to-do had candlesticks of silver as well as pewter, and they were burning candles made of a mixture of wax and tallow with cotton wicks. By the seventeenth century, candelabras had become popular, and were generously hung with cut glass pendants in a variety of shapes, including French-inspired designs from the glassworks at Baccarat.

In a wealthy home, a chandelier would be hung in the entrance, while wall sconces provided light in the bed chamber and the principal rooms. Expense was not spared with these gorgeous chandeliers, either – an average one was nearly a metre in diameter and made of decorative scrollwork in iron or wood. The Crusader was a popular motif in Tudor times and was often reproduced as ornamentation on candlesticks and chandeliers, symbolising the 'light' of the true faith.

From the seventeenth century onwards, candle sticks and candle holders were found at every social level, not just in the homes of the well-to-do. The materials used varied according to the status of the owner – from beautiful silver, brass, pewter, porcelain and even cut glass styles to simple tinplate (thin sheets of iron coated with tin to retard rusting) and wrought iron ones.

Moravian churches celebrate the birth of Jesus Christ on Christmas Eve with a 'Candle Love Feast'. Families attend church together, where food and drink are served, and special songs are sung. Each member of the congregation is given a lighted beeswax taper as a reminder to 'shine their light' for Jesus Christ in the coming year.

Much use was made of surface gilding, not only to prevent tarnishing and save the labour of polishing, but to give the candlestick an impressive appearance. By the early eighteenth century most candlesticks were shaped and ornamented so that they might take their place among the other decorative objects in a house, and the influence of the church and religious faith on the design came to an end.

For instance, in the eighteenth-century home of wealthy John Parker in Wiltshire, England, rooms were said to have been lit by candles in gorgeous tortoiseshell and ormulu candelabra on giltwood stands. In those days, candles had to be carried about the house because it was too expensive, too time-consuming and too downright dangerous just to keep them alight in upstairs rooms if no one was there. Servants placed the holders on the hall table for people to light their way upstairs to bed. A prudent eighteenth century lady, Mrs Whatman, observed in her household diary that, with the ever-present dangers of fire, 'the first thing a housekeeper should teach her new servant is to carry her candle upright'.

By the end of the seventeeth century it was also more common to find different types of candlesticks in homes, reflecting the different ways in which they were used – not just 'hand candlesticks' or 'chambersticks', but also table candlesticks and candle 'lamps', which had glass spheres around the candle flame, so as to increase the amount of light thrown by the flame. These were also much used in industry, particularly lace-making.

By the late 1850s, 'candle lanterns' were also widely available, these being tin lantern cases fitted with etched glass shades on four sides. These were often used to light barns or other outdoor buildings, and to light carriages. A novel invention from the 1890s was the Arctic Candle Lamp, a hollow metal tube with a candle inside: as the wick burnt down, a spring pushed the candle up, keeping the flame always in the same place. From these early designs came what we know today as the hurricane lantern or lamp.

Early candle lanterns usually featured a central spike onto which the candle was skewered. Later ones usually had the more familiar socket, almost always surrounded by a drip tray. Often they were inscribed with the initials of the owner and – in a hopeful attempt to discourage petty theft – with the name of a school, church or other institution. Occasionally household inventories list wooden or pottery candlesticks, but heavier metal ones have always been much more popular, for practical as well as aesthetic reasons. Most of the surviving candlesticks that we can enjoy looking at in museums today are made of metal, either precious or base. And, as an alternative to metal, glass and pottery were used from the mid-seventeenth century onwards, followed by porcelain.

Candle Holders

PINE CONE RING

This simple and attractive candle garland makes a wonderful festive table centrepiece.

YOU WILL NEED

About 6 small, well-formed pine cones
1 thick green candle
8–10 drops of essential oil of pine
Gold spray paint
Hot glue gun and glue sticks

METHOD

Sprinkle a few drops of pine oil over the pine cones. Spray the cones with gold paint, if desired.

Place the candle upright on a flat working surface and arrange the pine cones around the base of the candle. Dab the cones with hot glue and join them to form a firm circle that fits snugly around the base of the candle.

Safety note Never leave this candle unattended, and do not let it burn down right inside the pine cone ring, as there is the possibility that the cones could catch alight. If you are still concerned about flammability, omit the essential oil.

FLOWER POTS

You can buy terracotta flower pots of just about any size and shape these days, and they make terrific candle holders, being stable and fireproof, as well as lending themselves to all sorts of decorative possibilities. I like chunky, Mexican-style designs on flowerpots, using bright-coloured acrylic paints and simple geometric designs – zigzags and dots, for instance. If you're good at other painting styles, like folk art, this technique looks pretty, too.

One really simple trick is to just spray paint the inside of your terracotta pot with gold paint: when you light the candle inside, it really does glow beautifully.

If someone refers to a person as a 'candle holder', this is an old expression meaning that they are a helper, or abettor. The name comes from the Catholic Church's practice of having an assistant who holds a candle for the reader to see by. William Shakespeare also used the expression in Romeo and Juliet*: 'I'll be a candle-holder, and look on.'*

DECORATED TIN CANS

Even humble tin cans can be recycled and given a new lease of life as candle holders.

First, wash and dry the cans thoroughly and check for any rough edges. Then, give your imagination free rein. Don't try to be too dainty about decorating them: they are, after all, just cans! Running lengths of bright-coloured braid horizontally around the outside is one idea, or you can spray the cans gold or in a colour of your choice and use a hot glue gun to stick on fake jewels, sequins or cabochon-cut beads from your button box or craft shop.

IVY GARLANDS

A simple and dramatic way of decorating with candles is to use ivy. Ivy-decorated candles are especially appealing at Christmas time, whether it's in church or at home.

YOU WILL NEED

Tall slim cream candles
Fine florist's wire
Lengths of young, pliable ivy about 20–30 cm long (do not use woody or rooted ivy)

METHOD

Wind a length of ivy loosely around a candle to get an idea of how it will sit. Hold the ivy in place and, with your other hand, follow the ivy twist with a length of fine florist's wire. Secure it at the top and bottom with an extra twist of florist's wire.

Stand ivy-garlanded candles in plain, unobtrusive candle holders and arrange them in groups, with additional lengths of ivy around their bases.

Safety note Do not leave these candles unattended as the ivy is a fire risk. If they are to be lit and left burning for any period of time, simply snip off the uppermost piece of the length of ivy and the florist's wire.

FLORAL PEDESTAL

There are a multitude of ways in which you can combine flowers and candles to make gorgeous table centrepieces or arrangements for mantelpieces or buffets. A good tip for such arrangements is to display them in front of a mirror, which gives a glamorous effect and creates an illusion of size.

You will need

2 to 3 thick candles, of varying lengths
A cake pedestal, or purchased florist's pedestal vase
Mould seal or Plasticine
A piece of florist's Oasis cut to fit the bowl you are using
A selection of fresh flowers and ferns

Method

Hold a match or cigarette lighter to the base of each of the three candles to melt the wax, then turn them upright and press them into the desired positions on the pedestal, holding them still until they are firmly settled.

Cut or break the Oasis into curved chunks that will fit reasonably snugly around the base of the three candles. Soak the Oasis for several hours, or according to manufacturer's instructions. Arrange the flowers around the base of the candles, working so that all the pieces of Oasis are covered. Arrange longer pieces of foliage or flower stems, like fern or ivy, to drape gracefully over the sides. Mist the flowers well and place on table or buffet.

Safety note Do not leave these candles burning unattended, because the flowers (or the Oasis if it is left to dry out) might catch alight.

Glasses

Looking for a quick and inexpensive way to make a pretty decorative display in your home? Have a rummage through your glasses cupboard: glasses make simple, safe and very appealing candle holders. And they don't have to be expensive glasses. Look for short, straight-sided drinks glasses in thick green or blue glass, for instance, or even the cheap-and-cheerful embossed glasses you can buy in supermarkets.

You can either fill them with plain paraffin wax and drop in a wick, as I did for this book, or pop a tea-light inside each one, and group them in an attractive arrangement. And, if you've got time before the guests arrive, tie a ribbon around each or wire lengths of ivy round them.

Bottles

Don't stop just at the idea of the trusty old Chianti bottle seen in Italian restaurants!

If you have a collection of pretty bottles, you can easily create a beautiful display in a window or on a table by using them as candle holders. Even perfume bottles can be used by putting tiny birthday cake candles or Christmas tree candles in their necks.

Resources

NEW SOUTH WALES

Beads Galore
Shop 3, Metcalf Arcade
80 George Street
The Rocks NSW 2000
Ph: (02) 9247 5946
(beads, studs, decorative trims, pins)

The Craft Company
Shop 5, 272 Victoria Avenue
Chatswood NSW 2067
Ph: (02) 9413 1781
(moulds, wax, wicks, dyes)

Hornsby Bee-keeping Supplies
63a Hunter Street
Hornsby NSW 2077
Ph: (02) 9477 5569
(moulds, wax, wicks)

Janet's Art Supplies
145 Victoria Avenue
Chatswood NSW 2067
Ph: (02) 9417 8572
(moulds, wax, wicks, dyes)

John Guilfoyle
23 Charles Street
St Marys NSW 2760
Ph: (02) 9623 5585
(general craft supplier)

Mr Craft
Coolgun Lane
Eastwood NSW 2122
Ph: (02) 9858 2868
(general craft supplier)

QUEENSLAND

Pacific Wax Products
PO Box 129
Brisbane Markets Qld 4106
Ph: (07) 3274 3140
(moulds, wax, wicks, dyes, scents)

Queensland Handcrafts
36 Cordelia Street
South Brisbane Qld 4101
Ph: (07) 3844 5722
(moulds, wax, dyes)

The Wizard of the Wick
Unit 1, 40 Trinder Road
Ashgrove Qld 4060
Ph: (07) 3366 7003
(moulds, wax, wicks, dyes, scents)

SOUTH AUSTRALIA

Hope Valley Haberdashery & Craft
1220 Grand Junction Road
Hope Valley SA 5059
Ph: (08) 8396 2422
(wax, wicks)

TASMANIA

Hobart Craft Supplies
60 Liverpool Street
Hobart Tas. 7000
Ph: (03) 6231 3444
(wax, wicks, dyes, hardener)

VICTORIA

Allframes & Craft Supplies
Factory 22, 11 Havelock Road
Bayswater Vic. 3153
Ph: 9720 6276
(wax, wicks, dyes, hardener)

Bakerloo Trading Co Pty Ltd
236 Adderley Street
West Melbourne Vic. 3003
Ph: (03) 9328 1461
(wax, wicks, dyes, hardener)

Beads Galore
258 Chapel Street
Prahran Vic. 3181
Ph: (03) 9510 5477
(beads, studs, decorative trims, pins)

Handworks Supplies Pty Ltd
121 Commercial Road
South Yarra Vic. 3144
Ph: (03) 9820 8399
(wax, wicks, dyes, beads)

Norton Olympia Waxes
46 Renver Road
Clayton North Vic. 3168
Ph: (03) 9545 6333
(moulds, wax, dyes)

Scandles
Shop 219, Melbourne Central
300 Lonsdale Street
Melbourne Vic. 3000
Ph: (03) 9663 7174
(wax, wicks)

WESTERN AUSTRALIA

Meg Sheen Craftsman Supplier
308 Hay Street
Subiaco WA 6008
Ph: (09) 381 8215
(moulds, wax, wicks, dyes, hardener)

Lincraft and **Homecraft** stores in all states also supply candlemaking materials. Home decoration stores, such as **My House**, sometimes stock beeswax sheets, along with readymade candles and decorative trims, sequins, pearl beading and essential oils. Essential oils are also readily available from major department stores, health food shops and some pharmacies. Thermometers (candy or cooking) may be bought from kitchen supply shops and major craft suppliers. Major stationers are a good source of pins, glues, spray paint and poster paint, metal rulers, craft knives and the like.

Recommended reading

Eleanor Allen, *Home Sweet Home*, A & C Black (Publishers) Limited, London, 1979. (historical)

K. Lomneth Chisholm, *The Candlemaker's Primer*, Robert Hale & Company, London, 1974. (decorating/inspirational)

David J. Eveleigh, *Candle Lighting*, Shire Publications Ltd, Bucks, UK, 1985. (historical)

Marjorie Filbee, *A Woman's Place*, Ebury Press, London, 1980. (historical)

Valerie Janitch, *Candle Making and Decorations*, The Hamlyn Publishing Group, London, 1973. (decorating/inspirational)

Gloria Nicol, *The New Candle Book*, Hodder & Stoughton, Sydney, 1995. (decorating/inspirational)

Stanley Wells, *Period Lighting*, Pelham Books, London, 1975. (historical)

Geoffrey Wills, *Candlesticks*, David & Charles, Devon, UK, 1974. (historical)

Index

beads 43, 44
beeswax 6, 7, 8–9
beeswax candles 52–4
borax 12
bottles 61
buds *see* wax discs

candle holders 59–61
Candlemas 48
candlesticks 5, 56–8; *see also* candle holders
chandelier 56–8
chandlers 5–6
Chevreul, Michel Eugene 7
Christmas 38, 56, 60
Christmas tree candle 45–6
church 4, 50–1

dipped candle 14, 26–7
dye 12–13

eggshell candle 42–3
equipment 13–19

floating candle 31–2
flowers; drying 36; pots 59

glasses 61

Halloween 45
herb candle 41–2
holders *see* candle holders

ice candle 23–4

jewelled candle 44–5

lantern 58
lavender candle 39–40

medieval candle 48–50
melting point 8, 9
mosaic candle 46–8
moulds 9, 14, **15–18**, 28
mould seal 18–19

needle *see* wicking needle

oil, essential 13; palm 7; vegetable 21–2, 24

paint 30, 50
painted candle 29–31
palmatine 7
palm oil 7
paraffin wax 7, 8–9, *and throughout*
pine cone ring 59
plastic mould 9, 14, 15–17
pressed flower candle 36–7
priming (wick) 11–12

rose candle 34–6
rubber mould 9, 15–17
rush candle 4

safety 10
salt 12
sand candle 14, 15, 16, 24–5
scent 13
sequins 43, 44
shell candle 51–2
snuffer 32–3
spermaceti 6–7
starry candles 54–5
stearin 7, 8, **10–11**
stencilled candle 33–4
studded candle 43–4
superstitions 37–9

tallow 5, 6
taper 26
temperature 9, 14, 16, 24
thermometer 14–15, 24
tin cans 60
treasure candles 55–6
twisted candle 28–9

vegetable oil 21–2

wax **8–9**, *and throughout*; discs 12
wick 7, **11–12**, 33
wicking needle 15

64